Champagne Brunch

...a toast to Welcome Spring

Stuffed Baked Brie
French Toast with Strawberry Purée
Country Quiche
Sausage Muffins with Basil Honey
Cucumber Crescents
Lemon-Butter Muffins
Peach Jam
Sour Cream Coffee Cake
Baked Apricots
Rose-Geranium Sugar
Champagnes of your choice

Come quickly, I am tasting the stars!
- Dom Perignon, upon his discovery of champagne

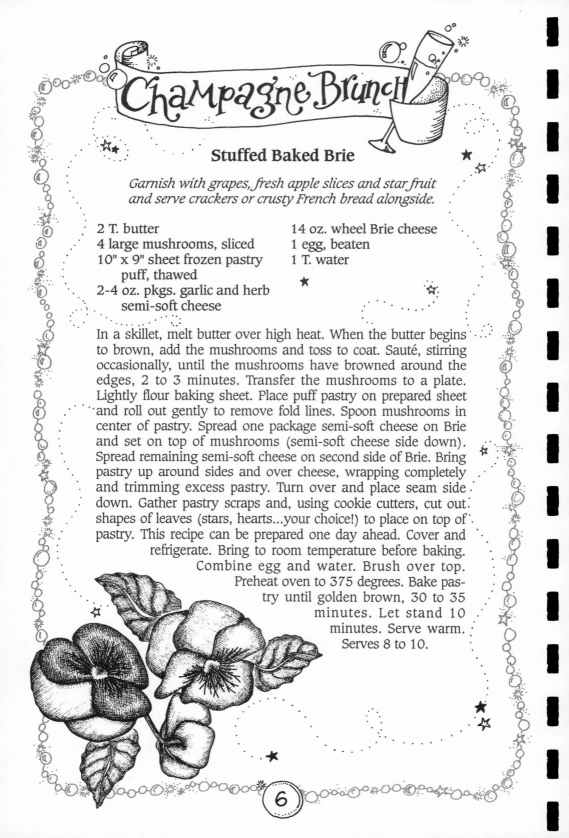

Champagne Brunch

Stuffed Baked Brie

*Garnish with grapes, fresh apple slices and star fruit
and serve crackers or crusty French bread alongside.*

2 T. butter
4 large mushrooms, sliced
10" x 9" sheet frozen pastry
   puff, thawed
2-4 oz. pkgs. garlic and herb
   semi-soft cheese

14 oz. wheel Brie cheese
1 egg, beaten
1 T. water

In a skillet, melt butter over high heat. When the butter begins
to brown, add the mushrooms and toss to coat. Sauté, stirring
occasionally, until the mushrooms have browned around the
edges, 2 to 3 minutes. Transfer the mushrooms to a plate.
Lightly flour baking sheet. Place puff pastry on prepared sheet
and roll out gently to remove fold lines. Spoon mushrooms in
center of pastry. Spread one package semi-soft cheese on Brie
and set on top of mushrooms (semi-soft cheese side down).
Spread remaining semi-soft cheese on second side of Brie. Bring
pastry up around sides and over cheese, wrapping completely
and trimming excess pastry. Turn over and place seam side
down. Gather pastry scraps and, using cookie cutters, cut out
shapes of leaves (stars, hearts...your choice!) to place on top of
pastry. This recipe can be prepared one day ahead. Cover and
refrigerate. Bring to room temperature before baking.
Combine egg and water. Brush over top.
Preheat oven to 375 degrees. Bake pastry until golden brown, 30 to 35
minutes. Let stand 10
minutes. Serve warm.
Serves 8 to 10.

Gooseberry Patch

A Country Store In Your Mailbox

Celebrate Spring

...fresh ideas
& garden
gatherings

A Country Store In Your Mailbox®

Gooseberry Patch
P.O. Box 190, Dept. CELS
Delaware, OH 43015
1-800-85-GOOSE
1-800-854-6673

Copyright 1997, Gooseberry Patch
1-888052-10-4
First Printing 30,000 copies, January, 1997

How To Subscribe

Would you like to receive
"A Country Store in Your Mailbox"℠?
For a 2-year subscription to our
Gooseberry Patch catalog
simply send $3.00 to:
Gooseberry Patch
P.O. Box 190, Dept. CELS
Delaware, OH 43015

Printed in the United States of America
TOOF COOKBOOK DIVISION

STARR ★ TOOF

670 South Cooper Street
Memphis, TN 38104

Contents

Dedication

Many thanks to all of our
Gooseberry Patch friends, who
inspire us every day of the year.

Appreciation

To anyone who has ever flown a kite,
planted a seed, picked a bouquet
of wildflowers or found joy in the first
warm breeze of spring.

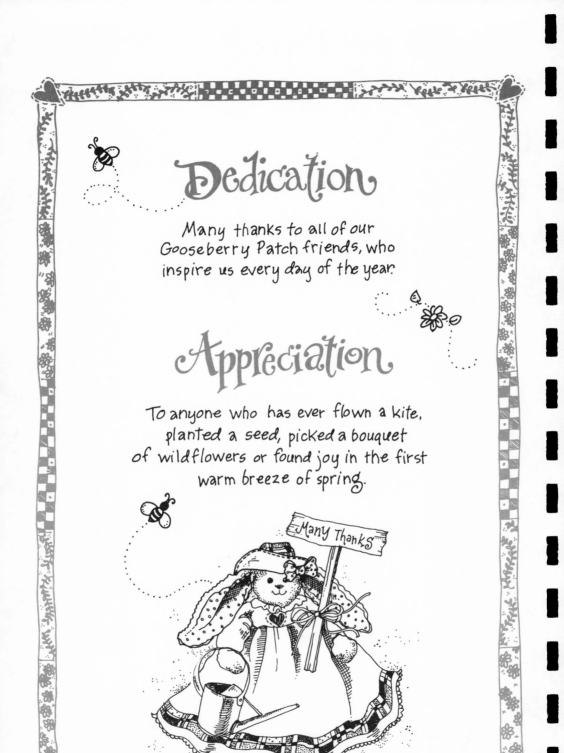

Many Thanks

French Toast with Strawberry Purée

Fresh, quick and elegant.

Purée:

1 pt. strawberries   sugar to taste (optional)

French Toast:

2 large eggs, whisked   1/8 t. nutmeg, ground
1/2 c. milk   1/2 t. vanilla extract
1/4 t. cinnamon   6 to 8 thin slices white bread

Purée berries and sugar together and set aside while preparing French toast.

Whisk together eggs, milk, cinnamon, nutmeg and vanilla. Thoroughly soak bread in mixture. Turn into a hot skillet and fry until both sides are golden and cooked through. Top with freshly prepared strawberry purée. Serves 2 or 3.

These I have loved:
White plates and cups, clean-gleaming,
Ringed with blue lines.
- Rupert Brooke

Strawberry Purée

Champagne Brunch

★ Country Quiche

A clever quiche that forms its own crust while baking.

3 eggs
1/2 c. biscuit mix
1/2 c. butter, melted
1 1/2 c. milk
1/4 t. salt

dash of pepper, freshly ground
1 c. Swiss cheese, shredded
1/2 c. smoked ham, cooked and cubed

Preheat oven to 350 degrees. Grease a 9-inch pie pan. Place all ingredients except cheese and ham in blender, and blend well. Pour mixture in pan. Sprinkle cheese and ham on top. Press gently below surface with back of spoon. Bake for 45 minutes. Let stand 10 minutes before cutting.

Berries, grapes and melon make a beautiful fruit cup when served in wine glasses.

Sausage Muffins with Basil Honey

Drizzle with our basil honey or your favorite herbal honey.

1/2 lb. ground pork or turkey
    sausage
2 c. all-purpose flour
2 T. sugar
1 T. baking powder
1/4 t. salt

1 c. milk
1 large egg, lightly beaten
1/4 c. butter or margarine,
    melted
1/2 c. cheddar cheese,
    shredded

Grease a muffin tin well with vegetable cooking spray. In a skillet, brown sausage and drain well; set aside. Combine flour, sugar, baking powder and salt and make a well in the center. Combine milk, egg and butter and add to dry mixture, mixing until just moistened. Stir in the sausage and cheese. Spoon batter into muffin tins, filling cups 2/3 full. Bake for 20 minutes or until golden brown. Remove from pans immediately. Makes one dozen.

Basil Honey:

1 c. honey
2 to 3 leaves fresh basil,
    finely chopped

Heat honey over low heat. Place basil in a jar or pot and pour in the warm honey. Cover tightly and allow to mellow for at least a week before using.

Champagne Brunch

Cucumber Crescents

Garnish with bright yellow spirals of lemon peel.

3 cucumbers, crescent-sliced
4 t. lemon juice
1 t. sugar
1/2 t. salt

3 T. butter, softened
1 T. basil, finely chopped
1 t. lemon zest

Using a vegetable peeler, scrape the cucumber skins off in channels lengthwise to form a striped pattern. Cut the cucumbers in half lengthwise; scoop out and discard the seeds. Cut seeded cucumbers into thin slices, making crescents. In a glass baking dish, toss cucumbers, three teaspoons of lemon juice, sugar and salt. Cover with vented wrap and microwave on high for 7 to 8 minutes, stirring once halfway through. In another dish, combine butter, basil, lemon zest and remaining teaspoon of lemon juice. To serve, transfer cucumbers to a serving plate and top with spoonfuls of lemon butter.

Where we love is home. Home that our feet may leave, but not our hearts.
- Oliver Wendell Holmes

Lemon-Butter Muffins

Luscious served with our peach jam.

1/2 c. fresh lemon juice
2 large eggs
2 T. lemon rind, freshly grated
1/2 c. butter, melted

2 c. all-purpose flour, unsifted
1/2 c. plus 2 T. sugar
1 T. baking powder
1 t. salt

Preheat oven to 400 degrees. Grease 2 muffin tins well. Stir lemon juice, eggs and lemon rind into melted butter. In another bowl, mix together flour, 1/2 cup sugar, baking powder and salt; make a well in the center. Stir in egg mixture and blend until well moistened. Pour into muffin tins, filling each cup about 2/3 full. Sprinkle tops of muffins with remaining 2 tablespoons of sugar. Bake for 15 to 20 minutes or until lightly browned. Makes 18-24 muffins.

Run a lemon wedge around the rims of glasses and dip in superfine sugar; garnish cool drinks with a sprig of mint.

Peach Jam

So easy to make, so rich and tangy. Keeps in the refrigerator for weeks.

1 lb. dried peaches   3 to 4 T. cognac
1/2 to 3/4 c. sugar

In heavy saucepan, cover peaches with water and simmer until it becomes a jam-like consistency. Stir in sugar and cognac to taste. Continue cooking over low heat until sugar is thoroughly dissolved and jam is thick. Let cool and refrigerate.

Serve luscious fruit sorbets in hollowed-out oranges, melon and pineapple halves.

Sour Cream Coffee Cake

A Midwestern favorite!

Nut filling:

1/3 c. brown sugar
1/4 c. white sugar

1 t. cinnamon
1 c. pecans, chopped

Cake:

1/2 c. butter
1 c. sugar
2 eggs
2 c. flour

1 t. baking powder
1/2 t. salt
1 c. sour cream
1 t. vanilla

Preheat oven to 350 degrees. Prepare nut filling by mixing all ingredients together; set aside. In another bowl, cream the butter. Add sugar gradually and cream until fluffy. Add eggs one at a time, beating well after each addition. Sift dry ingredients together and add to first mixture, alternating with sour cream and beginning and ending with flour. Mix in vanilla. Pour half of the mixture into greased 9"x5" loaf pan or 9-inch bundt pan. Cover with half of the nut filling and repeat. Bake for 40 to 50 minutes (loaf pan) or 70 minutes (bundt pan.)

When you plan your garden, plant flowers especially for making potpourri. Lavender, roses, violets, sweet peas and carnations, along with spices such as nutmeg, cinnamon and cloves, will make the ingredients for a variety of potpourris.

Champagne Brunch

Baked Apricots

A delicious dessert for brunch or supper. Try it on shortcake, topped with vanilla ice cream.

4 T. unsalted butter
1/2 c. rose-geranium sugar
(recipe follows)

8 ripe apricots, halved and pitted
1/2 c. heavy cream

Preheat oven to 375 degrees. Using half of the butter and rose-geranium sugar, line the bottom of a large baking dish. Layer the apricots (cut side down) in the dish, then top with remaining butter and sugar. Bake for 15 minutes. Remove from oven and add cream, pouring around fruit. Bake for another 5 minutes and serve warm.

Rose-Geranium Sugar

A lovely sweetener for iced tea or your breakfast oatmeal.

1 c. sugar
8 rose-geranium leaves

Mix sugar and leaves together and store tightly covered for at least one week. Remove leaves when ready to use.

A toast to welcome Spring

Fresh ideas...

Herb & Flower Drying Rack

An old-fashioned wooden windowpane frame makes a perfect herb rack. Remove the glass panes and paint the frame whatever color pleases you. Add a screw eye to each corner and thread heavy twine, fishing line or wire through the eyes. Affix hooks to your ceiling and hang your rack. Tie bundles of herbs and flowers upside down from the rack. After your flowers have air-dried, they should be placed in an air-tight container until ready to use in arrangements and craft projects.

Lavender Candle Ring

Coat an 8-inch straw wreath in white craft glue. Roll the wreath in dried lavender. Allow glue to set. Wind a narrow grosgrain ribbon around the wreath, allowing a length on either end to make a bow where the ends meet. Place your wreath on a small plate or saucer and add a pillar candle to the center. (You may want to coordinate the colors of ribbon and candle.)

Champagne Brunch

Herbal Bath Sachets

Mix a cup of dry oatmeal with 3/4 cup of powdered milk. Add a handful of dried lavender buds and another of dried rosemary flowers. You may add crushed peppermint leaves or violet petals as well. Stir ingredients. Place two teaspoons of the mixture in the center of a piece of gauze about 5" square. Cut off the ends with pinking shears and tie with a long, narrow ribbon. Hang the sachet under your running faucet for a luxurious bath.

Glass-Topped Art Gallery

This is the time of year when the kids bring home piles of artwork done during the school year. Select a small table or desk in your home for an ever-changing art gallery. Have a piece of glass cut to fit the top of the table. Then arrange your children's artwork under the glass. Encourages young artists, and makes a great conversation piece!

Champagne should be served chilled but not icy, to allow the delicate flavor to come through. Hold the glass by its stem to keep from warming it with your hands. Serve in tall flutes to preserve the bubbles longest.

Luck O' the Irish
...a wee bit o' the Emerald Isle

Boiled New England Dinner
Coddle
Colcannon
Potato Soup
Irish Soda Bread
Spinach Onion Casserole
Raspberry Crumble
Fruit Meringue Chantilly
Iced Shamrock Cookies
Old-Fashioned Rice Pudding

*The pedigree of honey
Does not concern the bee;
A clover, any time, to him
Is aristocracy.*
- Emily Dickinson

Luck O' the Irish

Boiled New England Dinner

Traditional Irish fare from Colonial days.

4 lbs. corned beef brisket, rinsed
6-8 carrots, peeled
8 medium-sized potatoes, peeled
6-8 small parsnips, peeled

1 head cabbage, cut into eighths
salt and pepper to taste
fresh parsley, chopped

In a large soup pot, cover beef brisket with water. Bring to a rolling boil for 5 minutes, removing the froth that comes to the surface. Reduce heat to very low and simmer, covered, 3 to 4 hours until meat is tender. Slice the vegetables and add to the water, cooking until tender. Season with salt and pepper and arrange meat and vegetables on a large platter, sprinkled with fresh chopped parsley.

★ Coddle

Serve this Irish dish steaming hot with fresh soda bread and butter.

8 thick slices ham or bacon, cubed
8 pork sausages
1 qt. boiling water
4 large onions, thinly sliced

2 lbs. potatoes, thinly sliced
4 T. fresh parsley, chopped
pinch of salt
freshly ground pepper to taste

Preheat oven to 250 degrees. Place the ham or bacon together with the sausages in boiling water for 5 minutes. Drain and reserve liquid. In a large baking dish combine onions, potatoes, parsley, seasonings and meat. Cover and bake for about and hour or until the liquid is reduced by half and all the ingredients are cooked but not mushy, basting occasionally.

Colcannon

The original Irish "comfort food."

1 lb. kale or white cabbage
   leaves, shredded
pinch of salt
1 lb. potatoes, unpeeled

6 scallions, finely chopped
2/3 c. milk or half and half
freshly ground pepper
4 to 6 T. butter, melted

Cook the kale or cabbage leaves in salted boiling water until very tender; approximately 10-20 minutes. Drain well and set aside. Cook the potatoes until tender, then drain and peel them. Return to heat and mash until very smooth; set aside. In small saucepan, combine onions and milk and simmer for about 5 minutes. Gradually add this liquid to the potatoes beating until fluffy. Mix in the cabbage and pepper. Heat thoroughly. Transfer to individual dishes, making a well in the center for melted butter.

*Did you ever eat colcannon
that's made from thickened cream,
with greens and scallions blended
like a picture in your dream?
Did you ever take potato cake
when you went off to school
tucked beneath your jacket
with your book and slate
and rule?*
- Irish children's rhyme

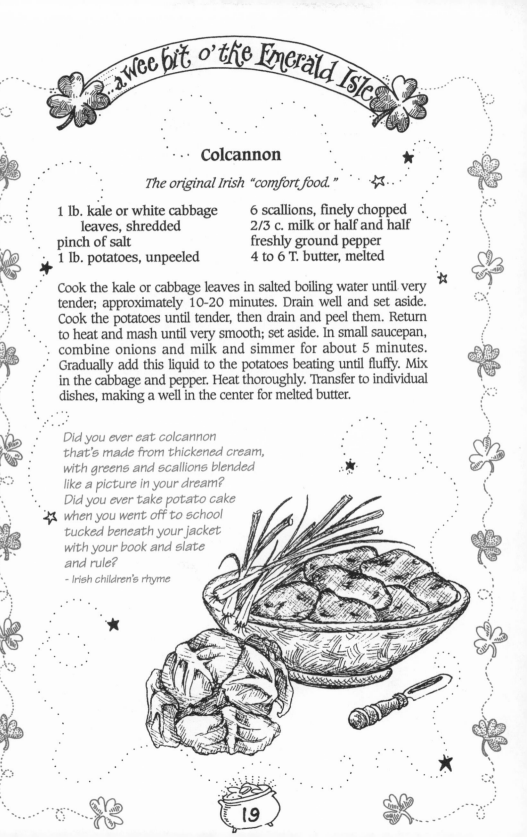

Luck O' the Irish

Potato Soup

We can never get enough potatoes!

2 large onions, finely
   chopped
4 T. butter
1 1/2 lb. potatoes, peeled
   and diced
salt and freshly ground
   pepper to taste

6 c. chicken stock
2 t. fresh chives, freshly
   chopped
milk (optional)

In large saucepan, sauté onion in butter until tender. Add potatoes, season with salt and pepper and mix together. Cook, covered, over low heat for about 10 minutes until tender. Add stock and bring to boil. Reduce heat and simmer for 20 to 30 minutes until the vegetables are tender. Remove from heat and allow to cool slightly. Transfer to a food processor or blender and purée until smooth. To serve, reheat gently. If soup is too thick, add a little extra stock or milk to desired consistency. Garnish with chives. Serves 6 to 8.

Irish Soda Bread

Serve with sweet butter, or try our herb butter recipe at the end of this chapter!

4 c. all-purpose flour   1 t. baking soda
1/2 t. salt   1 c. buttermilk

Preheat oven to 425 degrees. In mixing bowl, combine flour, salt and soda. Stir in buttermilk and mix to a soft dough consistency. Turn onto a floured work surface and knead lightly. Press out into a flat, round cake, about 2 inches high. Slice an "X" in the top. Place on a floured cookie sheet and bake for 30 to 40 minutes or until lightly browned. When done, it will sound hollow when tapped. Cool on wire rack. Makes one loaf.

May the roof above us never fall in,
and may we friends gathered here never fall out.
- Irish Blessing

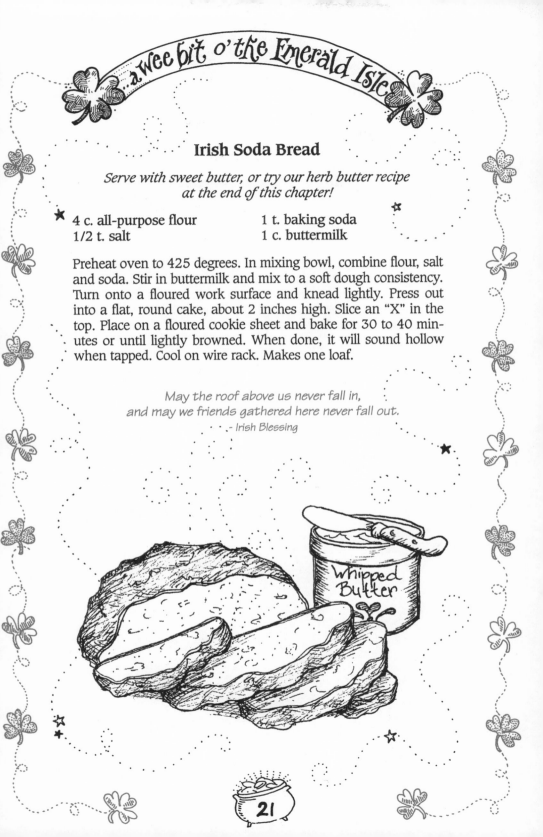

Luck O' the Irish

Spinach Onion Casserole

A quick, easy, company casserole.

1 1/4 lb. fresh spinach
1 envelope onion soup mix
1 pt. sour cream

2 T. sherry
1 small can French fried
  onion rings

Cook the spinach in a small amount of boiling salted water until limp. Drain and press out excess water. Combine spinach, soup mix, sour cream and sherry and spoon the mixture into a casserole dish. Bring to room temperature. Sprinkle with onions and bake in a 350 degree oven about 20 minutes, or until bubbling hot.

Faith, I wish I were a leprechaun
Beneath a hawthorn tree,
A-cobblin' wee, magic boots,
A-eatin' luscious, lovely fruits;
Oh fiddle-dum, oh fiddle-dee,
I wish I were a leprechaun
Beneath a hawthorn tree!
                    - Margaret Ritter

Raspberry Crumble

Top with freshly whipped cream.

1 lb. raspberries, rinsed   6 to 8 T. sugar

Topping:

1/2 c. butter or margarine   2/3 c. rolled oats
1 2/3 c. whole wheat flour   1/2 c. soft brown sugar

Preheat oven to 350 degrees. Line bottom of pie pan with raspberries and sprinkle sugar over them. In a mixing bowl, cut butter into flour and blend with pastry blender until crumbly. Stir in the oats and brown sugar and mix well. Sprinkle on top of the berries. Bake for 40 to 45 minutes until the top is golden.

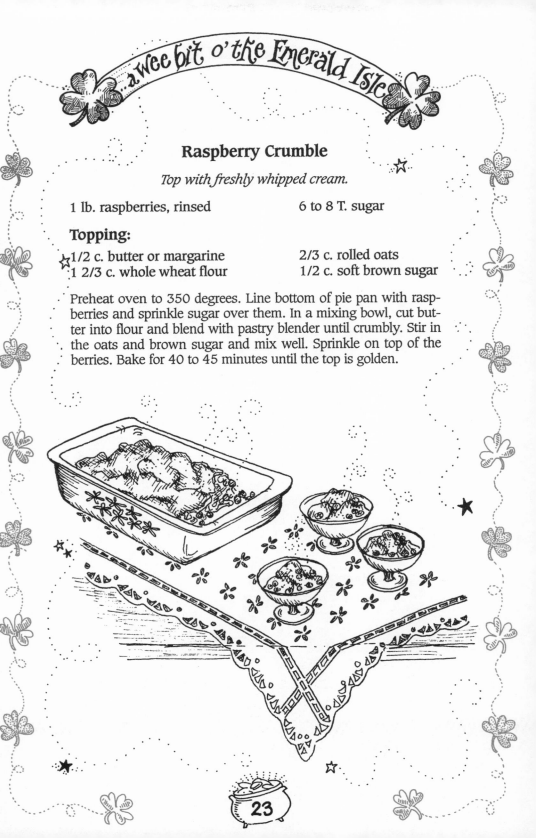

Luck O' the Irish

Fruit Meringue Chantilly

Fancy meringues were very popular in the olden days, and remain a New England treat!

1 1/2 c. egg whites, room temperature
3/4 t. cream of tartar
pinch of salt
2 1/4 c. granulated sugar
3 navel oranges, peeled and sectioned
1 banana, sliced, brushed with lemon juice

1 pineapple, peeled and cored
3/4 c. seedless green grapes
1/2 c. seedless purple grapes
1 kiwi fruit, peeled and sliced
3 c. heavy cream
3/4 c. powdered sugar
2 t. vanilla extract
2 oz. sweet chocolate, grated

Beat the egg whites with the cream of tartar and salt at high speed until stiff peaks are formed. Gradually beat in granulated sugar, checking to be sure meringue is still stiff with each addition of sugar. Drop spoonfuls of meringue onto two greased and floured baking sheets, about 1 1/4" apart. Bake in a preheated, 275 degree oven for one hour, until crisp. Cool on a wire rack. While meringues are baking, cut fruit into bite-sized pieces. Whip the heavy cream with the powdered sugar and vanilla. Fold fruit into the whipped cream. On a pretty platter, layer some of the meringues in a circle. Using the fruit and cream to stick the meringues together, continue layering the meringues to form a tree-shaped dessert. Garnish with fruit and sprinkle with chocolate. Serves 10.

Plant a fruit tree ... apple, peach, pear or plum. It will give you blossoms in springtime, shade in summer, luscious fruits in fall, and fragrant branches for firewood in winter.

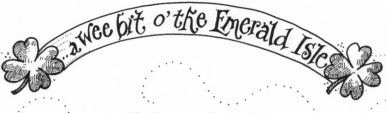
Iced Shamrock Cookies

A little fun on St. Patty's Day!

Cookies:

2 c. shortening
2 1/2 c. sugar
1 1/2 t. orange peel
1 1/2 t. vanilla
3 eggs

1/4 c. orange juice
6 c. flour
1 1/2 t. baking powder
3/4 t. salt

Cream shortening, sugar, orange peel and vanilla together. Add eggs and mix well. Add orange juice and mix again. Sift flour, baking powder and salt together and add to creamed mixture. Chill for two hours, covered. Roll on lightly floured surface 1/4 inch thick. Cut out three heart shapes for each shamrock and carefully stick them together. Cut out a long rectangle for the "stem." Bake at 375 degrees for 7-10 minutes. Allow to cool completely before removing from cookie sheet. Ice when cool.

Frosting:

1 c. powdered sugar
2 T. butter, softened
milk

peppermint extract to taste
3-4 drops green
food coloring

Combine sugar, butter and 2 tablespoons milk in a bowl and mix. Add peppermint extract to taste and food coloring to desired color. Add more milk if necessary, a teaspoon at a time, until frosting is smooth and spreadable. Sprinkle with fairy dust (crystallized sugar) if desired.

Luck O' the Irish

Old-Fashioned Rice Pudding

Bet you didn't know this is so simple and easy! Soak the raisins in rum for a special flavor.

1 T. butter
1/3 c. rice, washed and drained
pinch of salt

2 c. whole milk
1 T. sugar
1/4 c. raisins (optional)

Grease the bottom of a pie dish with butter. Mix together rice, salt, milk, sugar and raisins. Bake in a preheated 350 degree oven, stirring occasionally, for about 2 hours or until the rice is tender.

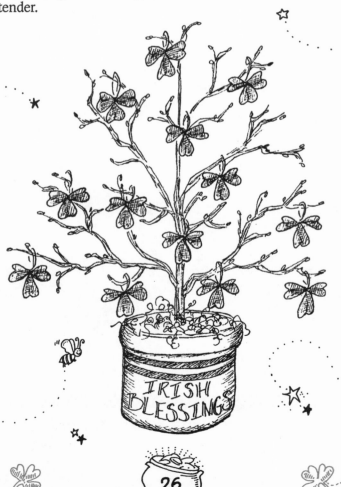

IRISH BLESSINGS

Shenanigans & Such...

Stenciled Shamrock Tablecloth

Using a heart cookie cutter, trace three hearts on a large piece of cardboard in the shape of a shamrock, adding a stem at the bottom. Be sure to leave at least 4 inches of margin around the shamrock. Cut out your shamrock with a sharp artist's blade. Position the stencil on a white cotton/polyester tablecloth and paint the inside design with permanent green acrylic paint. You may wish to make several sizes of shamrock stencils, and paint smaller ones in metallic gold for a magical touch. Use this same method for napkins, table runners, even T-shirts!

Tomorrow when the wind is high
I'll build a kite to ride the sky,
Tomorrow, when the wind is high.
—Rowena Bastin Bennett

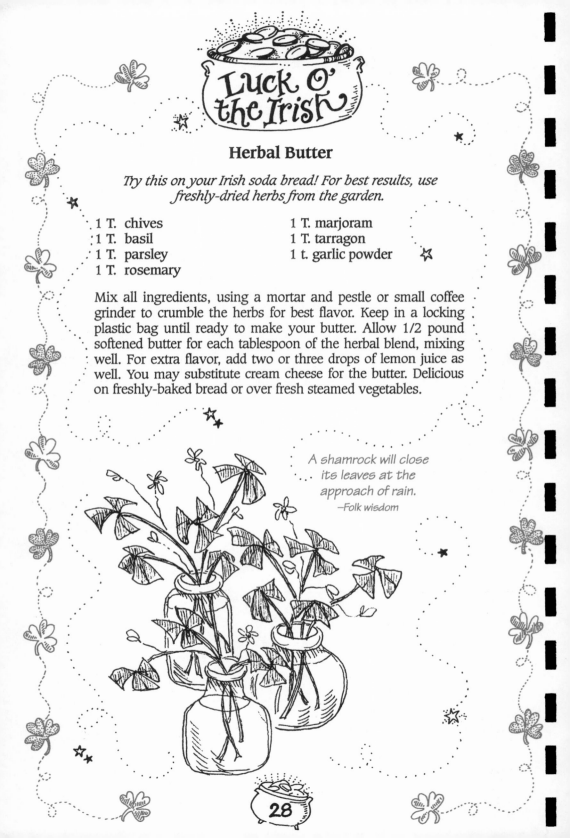

Luck O' the Irish

Herbal Butter

*Try this on your Irish soda bread! For best results, use
freshly-dried herbs from the garden.*

1 T. chives
1 T. basil
1 T. parsley
1 T. rosemary

1 T. marjoram
1 T. tarragon
1 t. garlic powder

Mix all ingredients, using a mortar and pestle or small coffee
grinder to crumble the herbs for best flavor. Keep in a locking
plastic bag until ready to make your butter. Allow 1/2 pound
softened butter for each tablespoon of the herbal blend, mixing
well. For extra flavor, add two or three drops of lemon juice as
well. You may substitute cream cheese for the butter. Delicious
on freshly-baked bread or over fresh steamed vegetables.

*A shamrock will close
its leaves at the
approach of rain.*
—Folk wisdom

Spring Buffet

...Sunday's best

Mushroom Turnovers
Spinach-Cheese Squares
Spring Pea Soup
Roast Lamb with Plum Sauce
Baked Country Ham
Chicken Piquant with Pinot Noir Sauce
Fresh Asparagus with Tomato Vinaigrette
Rice Pilaf with Carrots
Blackberry-Peach Crisp
Springtime Cake Roll

I meant to do my work today—
But a brown bird sang in the apple tree,
And a butterfly flitted across the field,
And all the leaves were calling me.

And the wind went sighing over the land,
Tossing the grasses to and fro,
And a rainbow held out its shining hand
So what could I do but laugh and go?
—Richard LeGallienne

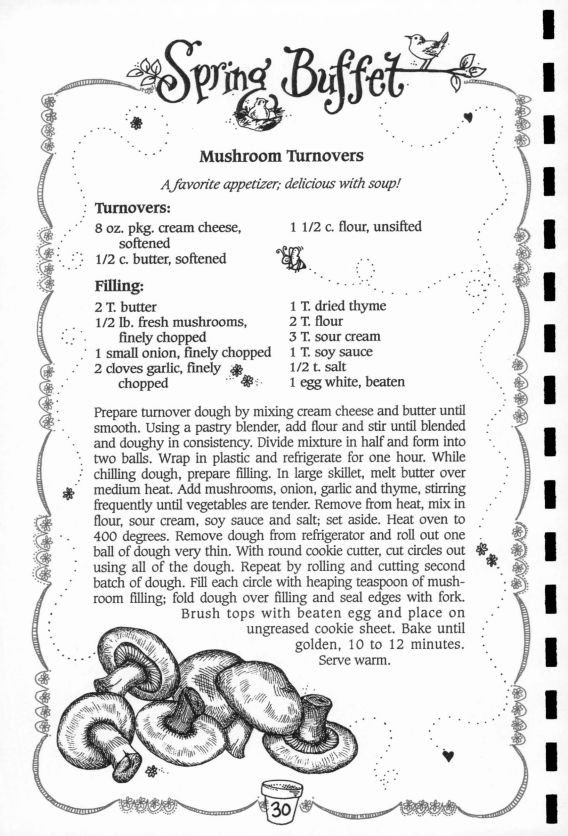

Spring Buffet

Mushroom Turnovers

A favorite appetizer; delicious with soup!

Turnovers:

8 oz. pkg. cream cheese, softened

1/2 c. butter, softened

1 1/2 c. flour, unsifted

Filling:

2 T. butter
1/2 lb. fresh mushrooms, finely chopped
1 small onion, finely chopped
2 cloves garlic, finely chopped

1 T. dried thyme
2 T. flour
3 T. sour cream
1 T. soy sauce
1/2 t. salt
1 egg white, beaten

Prepare turnover dough by mixing cream cheese and butter until smooth. Using a pastry blender, add flour and stir until blended and doughy in consistency. Divide mixture in half and form into two balls. Wrap in plastic and refrigerate for one hour. While chilling dough, prepare filling. In large skillet, melt butter over medium heat. Add mushrooms, onion, garlic and thyme, stirring frequently until vegetables are tender. Remove from heat, mix in flour, sour cream, soy sauce and salt; set aside. Heat oven to 400 degrees. Remove dough from refrigerator and roll out one ball of dough very thin. With round cookie cutter, cut circles out using all of the dough. Repeat by rolling and cutting second batch of dough. Fill each circle with heaping teaspoon of mushroom filling; fold dough over filling and seal edges with fork. Brush tops with beaten egg and place on ungreased cookie sheet. Bake until golden, 10 to 12 minutes. Serve warm.

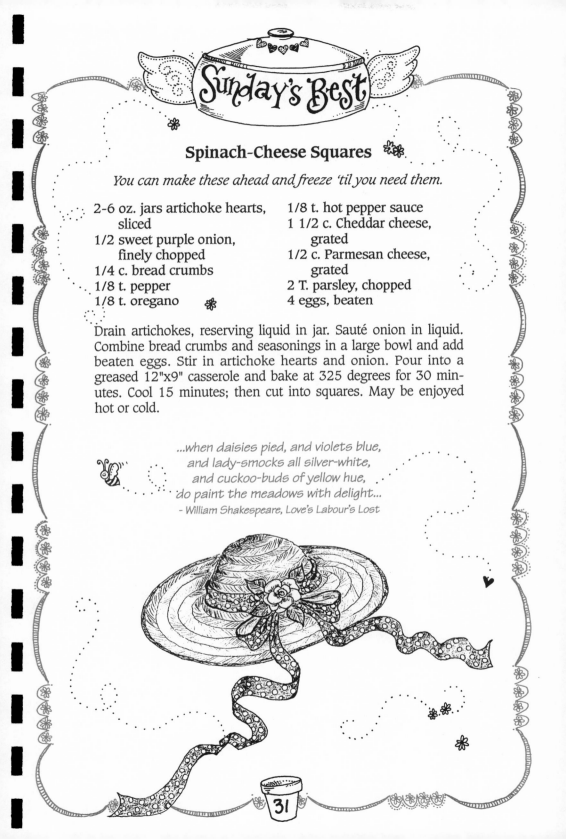

Sunday's Best

Spinach-Cheese Squares

You can make these ahead and freeze 'til you need them.

2-6 oz. jars artichoke hearts,
   sliced
1/2 sweet purple onion,
   finely chopped
1/4 c. bread crumbs
1/8 t. pepper
1/8 t. oregano

1/8 t. hot pepper sauce
1 1/2 c. Cheddar cheese,
   grated
1/2 c. Parmesan cheese,
   grated
2 T. parsley, chopped
4 eggs, beaten

Drain artichokes, reserving liquid in jar. Sauté onion in liquid. Combine bread crumbs and seasonings in a large bowl and add beaten eggs. Stir in artichoke hearts and onion. Pour into a greased 12"x9" casserole and bake at 325 degrees for 30 minutes. Cool 15 minutes; then cut into squares. May be enjoyed hot or cold.

...when daisies pied, and violets blue,
and lady-smocks all silver-white,
and cuckoo-buds of yellow hue,
do paint the meadows with delight...
- William Shakespeare, Love's Labour's Lost

31

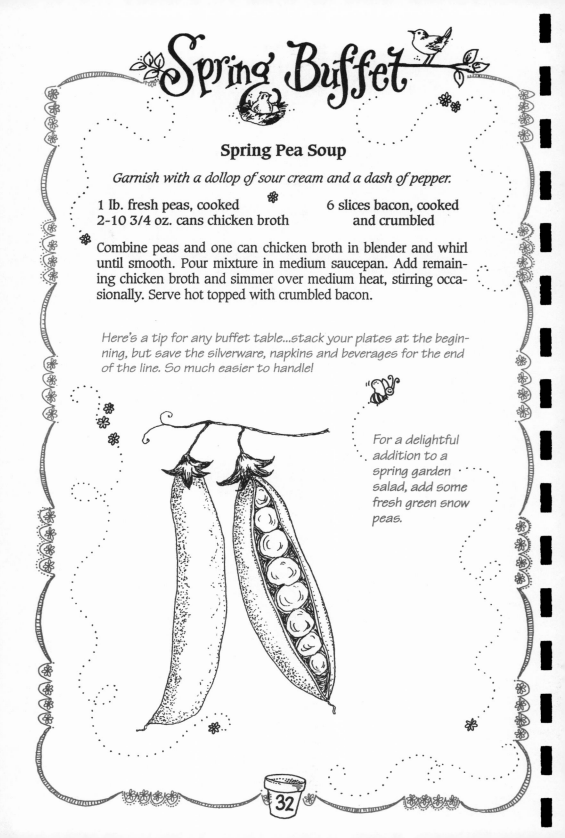

Spring Buffet

Spring Pea Soup

Garnish with a dollop of sour cream and a dash of pepper.

1 lb. fresh peas, cooked
2-10 3/4 oz. cans chicken broth

6 slices bacon, cooked
and crumbled

Combine peas and one can chicken broth in blender and whirl until smooth. Pour mixture in medium saucepan. Add remaining chicken broth and simmer over medium heat, stirring occasionally. Serve hot topped with crumbled bacon.

Here's a tip for any buffet table...stack your plates at the beginning, but save the silverware, napkins and beverages for the end of the line. So much easier to handle!

For a delightful addition to a spring garden salad, add some fresh green snow peas.

Roast Lamb with Plum Sauce

A springtime tradition.

4 to 5 lb. leg of lamb	1 t. celery salt
1 clove garlic, halved	1/2 t. pepper
1 T. parsley, snipped	1/4 t. paprika
1 t. salt	

Rub leg of lamb all over with cut side of garlic; discard garlic. Combine parsley, salt, celery salt, pepper and paprika and rub into meat. Place lamb, fat side up, on a rack in a shallow roasting pan. Insert meat thermometer in the thickest portion of meat. Roast for about 3 hours or until thermometer registers 175 to 180 degrees.

Plum Sauce:

3/4 c. plum jelly	1 T. orange juice
1/4 c. unsweetened pineapple juice	1/4 T. dry mustard
1 T. cornstarch	dash of mace

In a small saucepan combine plum jelly, pineapple juice, cornstarch, orange juice, dry mustard and mace. Cook and stir until thickened and bubbly. Cook and stir 2 minutes more. Serve with roast lamb.

Baked Country Ham

Score the fat in a diamond pattern.
Stick whole cloves into the center of each diamond.

8 - 10 lb. cured Virginia ham
2 T. prepared mustard

1 c. dark brown sugar
1/2 c. honey
cloves

Put the ham in a large Dutch oven and cover with cold water. Let soak for 24 hours. Pour off water, cover with fresh cold water and bring to a simmer over medium heat. Remove from heat and set ham aside to cool. Preheat oven to 350 degrees. Remove skin from the ham. Score and place in a roasting pan on a rack. Bake about 3 to 3-1/2 hours (20 minutes per pound). Combine mustard, brown sugar and honey in a bowl. Spread mixture over the ham; then stud with cloves. Raise oven temperature to 450 degrees and bake ham for 30 minutes longer.

The most remarkable thing about my mother is that for thirty years she served the family nothing but leftovers. The original meal has never been found.

- Calvin Trillin

For an extra special spring welcome, place a potted lily by your front door on Easter Day.

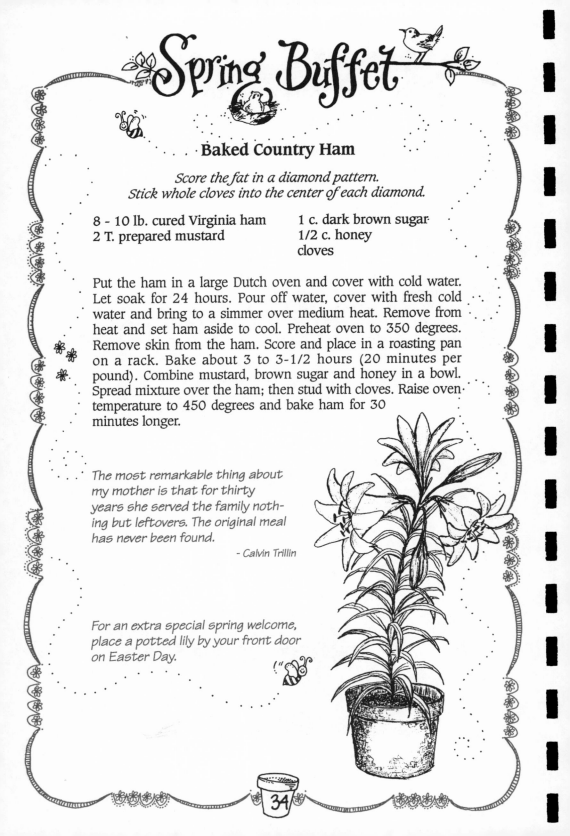

Chicken Piquant with Pinot Noir Sauce

Another festive choice for Easter or any special occasion.

4 skinless, boneless chicken
   breasts, cut into strips
1 bottle Pinot Noir (dry white
   wine)
3 garlic cloves, peeled and
   sliced
2 T. sugar
1/2 c. plus 1 T. raspberry
   vinegar

1 T. olive oil
salt and freshly ground
   pepper
5 T. butter, divided
1/4 lb. fresh mushrooms,
   sliced
fresh raspberries and grapes
   for garnish

Marinate chicken in 2 cups wine for at least 1 hour. Meanwhile combine garlic, sugar, 1/2 cup wine and 1 tablespoon raspberry vinegar in saucepan. Bring to boil over high heat, dissolving sugar. Reduce heat, cover and cook until garlic is tender, about 12 minutes. Uncover, increase heat to high. Cook until liquid is reduced to a thick syrup and the garlic is glazed, approximately 10 to 15 minutes. Stir in remaining raspberry vinegar. Heat oil and one tablespoon butter in skillet. Sauté chicken until cooked. Set aside. Sauté mushrooms in same skillet. Remove to a platter with chicken. Add sauce to skillet. Cook on high until syrupy. Stir in remaining 4 tablespoons butter, salt and pepper. Return chicken and mushrooms to skillet. Toss gently until heated through. Arrange chicken on platter and pour sauce with mushrooms over the chicken. Garnish with red raspberries and grapes.

Spring Buffet

Asparagus with Tomato Vinaigrette

Just hold the asparagus by both ends and snap off the woody stems...they'll naturally break right where they should!

1/2 t. salt
1 lb. fresh asparagus
3 T. virgin olive oil

1 1/2 T. white wine vinegar
1/2 t. honey
2 large tomatoes, seeded and
    chopped

Cover bottom of medium saucepan with about 1 inch of water and bring to rolling boil. Add salt and asparagus and boil for about 3 to 5 minutes, until tender. Drain. In another saucepan, heat olive oil and stir in vinegar and honey. Add tomatoes and heat through. To serve, pour tomato vinaigrette over asparagus.

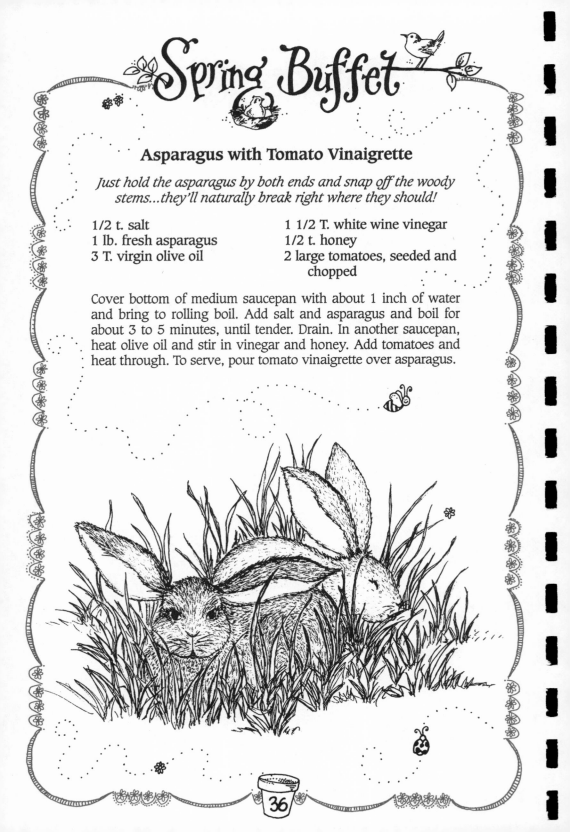

Rice Pilaf with Carrots

Delicious, low-fat and perfect with chicken dishes!

1 T. vegetable oil	1/2 t. salt
2 c. basmati rice, uncooked	1 c. fresh carrots, finely
1/4 c. onion, chopped	chopped
2 cloves garlic, minced	1/2 c. green onions, chopped
4 c. chicken broth	3 T. pine nuts, toasted

Heat oil in a medium saucepan over medium-high heat. Add rice and onion; sauté 2 minutes. Add the garlic; sauté 1 minute. Add broth and salt; bring to a boil. Cover, reduce heat, and simmer 7 minutes. Stir in carrots; cover and cook and additional 7 minutes or until liquid is absorbed. Remove from heat; stir in remaining ingredients. Let stand covered for 5 minutes, then fluff with a fork. Serves 7.

To make an Easter basket cake, decorate the top of a white layer cake with green-colored coconut. Arrange jelly beans on top; then insert both ends of a long chenille wire into the cake to form the basket "handle." Twine silk flower stems around the handle.

DEAR BUNNY
PLEASE
HOP HERE

Spring Buffet

Blackberry-Peach Crisp

Top with vanilla ice cream or frozen yogurt!

Fruit:

3 lbs. peaches, pitted and cut
    into 1/2" wedges
6 c. fresh blackberries

1 1/2 c. sugar
2 T. instant tapioca

Combine all ingredients in a large bowl and toss until sugar and tapioca are well mixed throughout. Let stand 15 minutes. Transfer fruit mixture to a 13"x9" baking dish. Prepare topping (see below) and sprinkle topping over fruit. Bake in a 375 degree oven until brown and bubbly, about 50 minutes. Allow to cool slightly before serving.

Topping:

1 1/4 c. old-fashioned
    oatmeal
1c. plus 2 T. brown sugar,
    firmly packed
3/4 c. flour

1 T. lemon peel, grated fine
3/4 c. sweet butter

Combine all ingredients except butter in a food processor. Gradually add butter and cut in, using pulse button, until you have a coarse crumb mixture.

Sunday's Best

Springtime Cake Roll

Display on a pretty tray garnished with candied spring flowers.

Orange filling:

1/3 c. sugar
1/4 c. cornstarch
1 c. fresh orange juice
2 T. fresh lemon juice

1 t. grated orange zest
1 large egg, beaten
2 T. butter, softened
edible flowers and prepared
    whipped cream as garnish

Combine sugar and cornstarch in a medium saucepan. Blend in the juices and the zest and cook over medium heat, stirring constantly, until mixture thickens. Continue to cook and stir for about 5 minutes. Remove from heat and add a portion of it to the beaten egg, whisking until smooth. Return the egg mixture to the juice mixture and cook for a few minutes longer over low heat. Stir in the butter, then remove from heat and allow to cool.

Cake roll:

1 c. flour
1 t. baking powder
1/2 t. salt
3 large eggs, room temperature

1 t. vanilla extract
1 c. sugar
1/3 c. hot water
powdered sugar

Whisk together the flour, baking powder and salt in a medium bowl. In a separate bowl, beat eggs and vanilla with a mixer and add the sugar, a bit at a time, beating for about another minute. Reduce mixer speed and add flour mixture to the egg mixture until blended. Do not overbeat. Add the hot water and mix again until batter is smooth. Spread in a 15"x10" jelly roll pan that has been lined with foil and greased. Bake for 12-14 minutes at 375 degrees. Loosen cake with a knife and sift the powdered sugar over the top. Cover the cake with a clean tea towel and invert onto a flat surface. Remove the towel and the foil, cutting off any brown edges. Using the towel, roll up the cake and towel together. Transfer to a rack and cool completely. Unroll the cake and spread with most of the orange filling, reserving 1/3 of the filling for frosting. Roll the cake up again and transfer to a serving platter. Frost with the remaining filling and garnish with whipped cream and bright, fresh nasturtiums, violets or pansies.

Spring Buffet

Springy things...

Eggshell Vase

Take a large raw egg and carefully prick a small hole, about 1/4-inch in diameter, in one end with a large needle. Prick a needle-sized hole in the other end. Blow through the smaller hole until the contents of the egg have drained out. Rinse the egg with clear water and dry. Seal the smaller hole with glue. Carefully dye the shell a pretty Easter egg color, such as lavender, buttercup yellow or soft rose. Fill the eggshell with water and a tiny bouquet of pansies. Set in a china egg cup or tiny terra cotta pot.

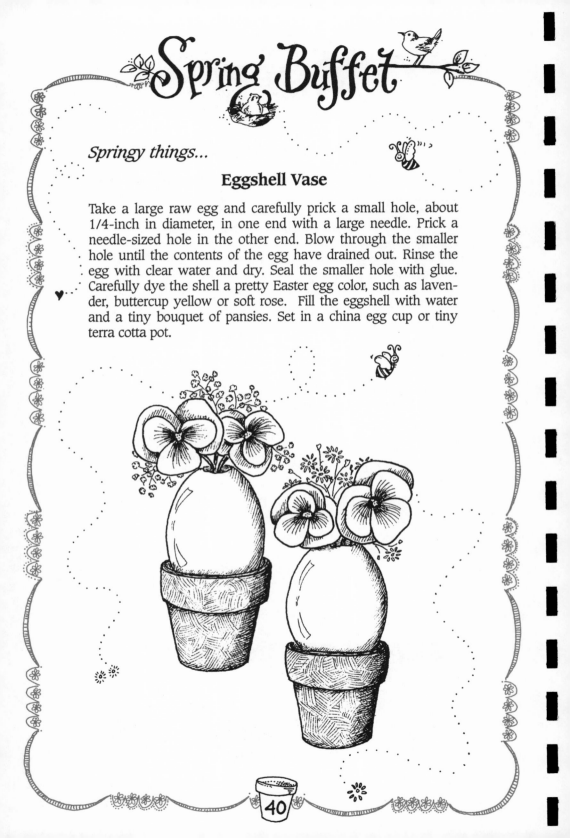

Candied Flowers

Edible flowers such as pansies, violets, roses and forget-me-nots look beautiful when crystallized in sugar. Select very fresh flowers, and process them immediately after picking. Cut the stem off very short. Add some water to egg white and brush all over the flower with a small artist's brush. (You'll want to hold the blossom very gently by the stem with a pair of tweezers.) With a shaker, sprinkle superfine white sugar all over the flower. Place on a sheet of waxed paper and allow to set for at least 48 hours, turning if necessary to allow the drying to take place. Use your candied flowers to decorate a centerpiece or cake top.

Note: If you wish to make edible candied flowers, you may want to use meringue powder mixed with water instead of the raw egg white. You can find meringue powder at baking specialty shops.

Lattice Herb Hanger

You can find a piece of unfinished wooden lattice at garden and home stores. With wall paint, paint the lattice a color to complement the kitchen of your home, adding stencils or hand-painted designs of your choice. Now you can be creative about what type of hooks you want on your hanger...you'll find a variety of wooden pegs, brass hooks and ornamental knobs at the hardware store. Hang on the wall and use to display bundles of herbs and dried flowers.

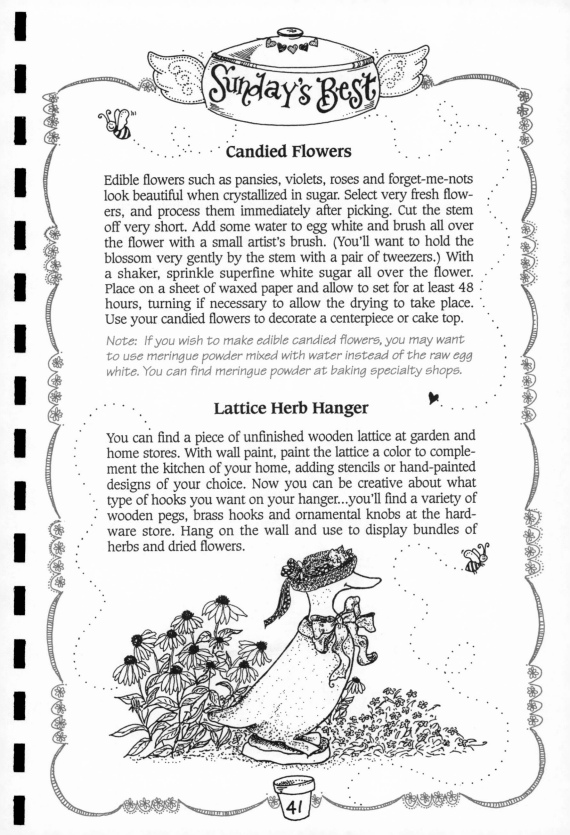

Spring Buffet

Decorated Eggs

This year, dye your eggs the natural way. Use slightly mashed blackberries, coffee, grass or raw beets for a variety of colors. Put hard-boiled eggs in a saucepan and cover with the ingredients of your choice, then cover with water and add a tablespoon of vinegar. Simmer for 20 minutes; remove from heat and allow colors to sit in the water for about an hour. Drain eggs and air dry on a rack (with paper towels underneath). For a glossy finish, brush with a little vegetable oil when dry. ♥

When was the last time you colored Easter eggs? This year, why not host a "grown-ups only" egg-coloring party? Have prizes on hand for the most colorful, best decorated and funniest eggs.

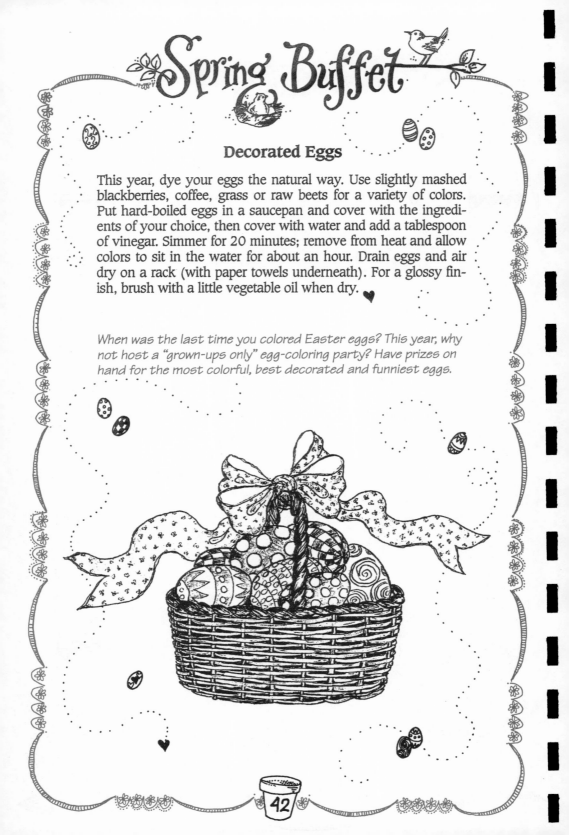

Romantic Dinner
...you for me & me for you

Chicken with Tarragon Cream
Potato Pie with Peppers
Mandarin Orange, Spinach and Almond Salad
Baked Basil Tomatoes with Artichoke Hearts
Blueberry Delight
Chocolate Cappucino Brownies

The Meanings of Flowers
Acacia...secret love
Camellia...excellence
Carnation...distinction
Forget-me-not...true love
Daisy...innocence
Gardenia...joy
Honeysuckle...devotion
Ivy...marriage, fidelity
Lily...purity
Lily-of-the-valley...happiness
Orange blossom...loveliness and happiness
Rosemary...remembrance
Pansy...shyness
Rose...love

You're invited

Romantic Dinner

Chicken with Tarragon Cream

Looks beautiful garnished with thin slices of lemon and sprigs of parsley.

2 T. butter, melted
4 skinless, boneless chicken breasts
1 c. chicken broth
1/4 c. shallots, chopped
1 t. dried tarragon, crushed

3/4 c. whipping cream
1 t. fresh lemon juice
1/2 t. grated lemon peel
pepper to taste

Place butter in large skillet. Add chicken and cook until lightly browned. Stir in broth, then add shallots and tarragon. Cover and simmer for about 10 minutes. Remove chicken (keeping it warm on serving platter.) Boil remaining juices until a half cup remains. Add cream and cook until smooth, stirring constantly, about 5 minutes. Mix in lemon juice and peel. Season sauce with freshly ground pepper and pour over chicken.

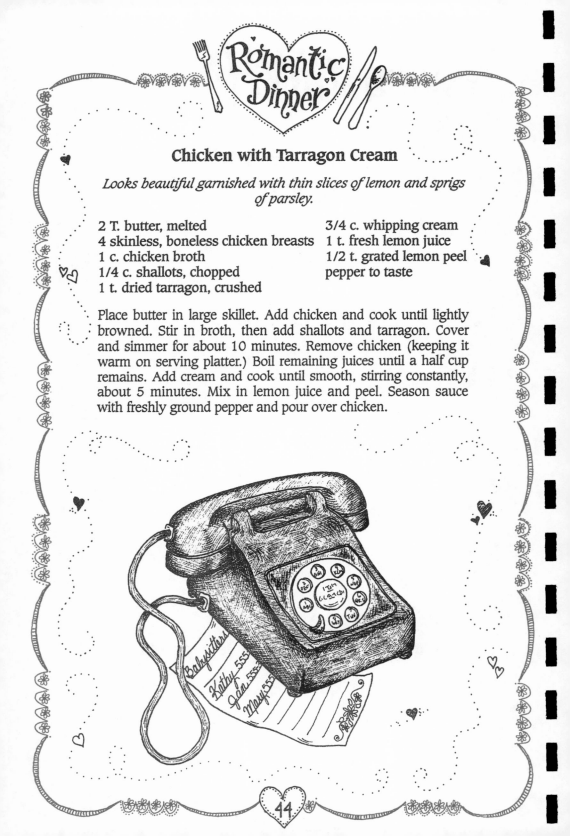

Potato Pie with Peppers

If you like a little spice, add some hot pepper flakes to your potatoes.

2 lbs. russet potatoes, peeled and sliced
1 large onion, peeled and sliced thinly
1/4 c. olive oil
1/4 c. fresh basil, minced

2 t. salt
freshly ground pepper to taste
2 large peppers, one red and one yellow, diced
8 phyllo pastry leaves, buttered

Combine the potatoes, onion, oil, basil, salt and pepper and set aside. Unroll the phyllo dough and brush with butter. Line a tart pan with the leaves, folding them in half and overlapping them in the center of the pan so they look like spokes in a wheel. The dough will overhang the sides of the pan. Transfer the potato mixture into the pan and top with the diced peppers. Lift the ends of each pastry leaf up over the potatoes in a pinwheel pattern until the potatoes are covered. Brush with melted butter and bake in a 350 degree oven for about 90 minutes. Serves 6.

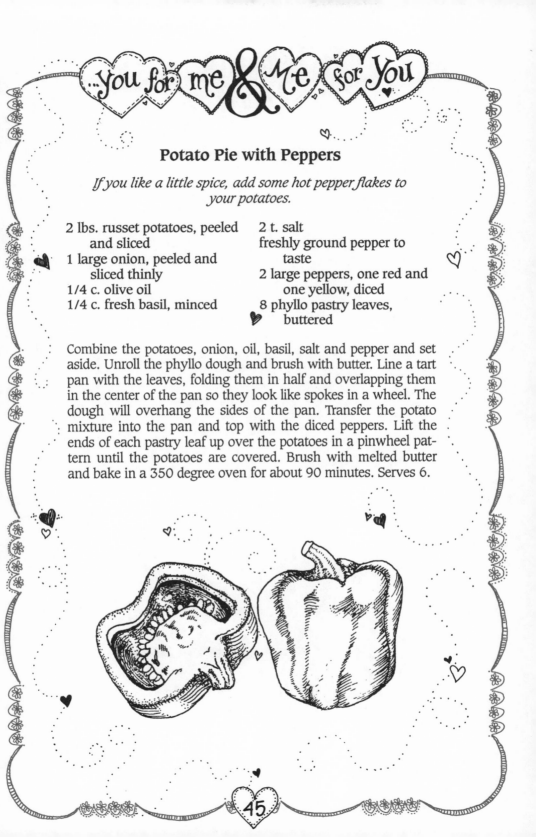

Romantic Dinner

Here's a romantic idea for anniversaries or birthdays...

Just for fun, send your spouse on a scavenger hunt at the mall! Select special little gifts at various shops...a few chocolate truffles at the candy shop, bubble bath or shaving cream at a bath shop, a favorite tape at the music store and so on. At each store leave a note on the gift-wrapped pre-paid package sending them to the next stop. End the day by meeting at a favorite restaurant.

Curlylocks, Curlylocks,
Will you be mine?
You need not wash dishes
Nor feed the swine,
But sit on a cushion
And sew a fine seam,
And feed upon strawberries
Sugar and cream.
- Old children's rhyme

...you for me & Me for You

Mandarin Orange, Spinach and Almond Salad

A colorful spring salad, crunchy and different!

10 oz. bag fresh spinach,
    washed and drained
11 oz. can mandarin
    oranges, 2 T. juice
    reserved

1/2 c. extra virgin olive oil
3 T. balsamic vinegar
1/4 c. honey roasted
    almond slivers

In a salad bowl, combine spinach and mandarin oranges. In another bowl, whisk together olive oil, vinegar and mandarin orange juice. Pour the dressing over the spinach and oranges and toss gently. Top with almonds.

The way to love anything is to realize that it might be lost.
- G.K. Chesterton

Romantic Dinner

Baked Basil Tomatoes with Artichoke Hearts

*If vine-ripened tomatoes aren't available, substitute
2 pounds of Roma tomatoes.*

1 stick butter or margarine
1/2 c. onion, finely chopped
2 T. shallots, finely chopped
4 large red tomatoes, sliced
14 oz. can artichoke hearts,
   drained and rinsed

1/2 t. leaf basil
2 T. sugar
salt and freshly ground
   pepper to taste

Preheat oven to 325 degrees. In melted butter or margarine, sauté onion and shallots until tender. Add tomatoes, artichoke hearts and basil, stirring gently about 2 minutes. Stir in sugar, salt, and pepper. Pour into greased casserole dish and bake until vegetables are heated through, about 10 to 15 minutes.

*Gather ye rosebuds while ye may,
Old Time is still a-flying;
And this same flower that smiles today
Tomorrow will be dying.*
   - Robert Herrick

...you for me & Me for you

Blueberry Delight

A creamy-light, chilled dessert.

1/2 c. sugar	3/4 c. butter, melted
1/4 c. cornstarch	16 oz. cream cheese, softened
3 c. fresh blueberries	1 1/2 c. sugar
1/2 c. water	2 t. vanilla
2 c. graham cracker crumbs	1 c. whipping cream, whipped

Combine 1/2 cup sugar with the cornstarch in a medium saucepan. Add the blueberries and water. Cook over medium heat until bubbly, stirring constantly. Simmer and stir for 2 minutes more. Remove from heat, cover and set aside to cool. Combine graham cracker crumbs and butter and set aside half of the mixture for topping. Press the remaining half of the mixture into the bottom of a 13"x9" glass baking dish. In a medium bowl, beat cream cheese, 1 1/2 cups sugar and vanilla. Fold in whipped cream. Spoon half of the cream cheese mixture over the crust. Spoon blueberry mixture over cream cheese mixture. Top with remaining cream cheese mixture. Sprinkle crumbs over all. Chill, covered, at least 2 hours. Serves 10-12.

Chocolate Cappuccino Brownies

Chewy and chocolatey together...delicious!

1/2 c. butter
1 c. brown sugar
2 T. instant coffee powder
3 eggs
1 t. vanilla
1 t. baking powder

1/2 t. salt
1 1/4 c. unbleached white
  flour, sifted
6 T. cocoa powder
1/2 c. brewed coffee, cooled
1 c. walnuts, chopped
1 c. semi-sweet chocolate
  chips

Melt the butter and add the brown sugar and coffee powder; blend well. Add the eggs, vanilla, baking powder and salt and stir. Combine with flour, cocoa powder and coffee. Add nuts and chips. Pour batter into a 13"x9" pan and bake at 350 degrees for 25 to 30 minutes. Allow to cool and cut into squares. Makes 18-24.

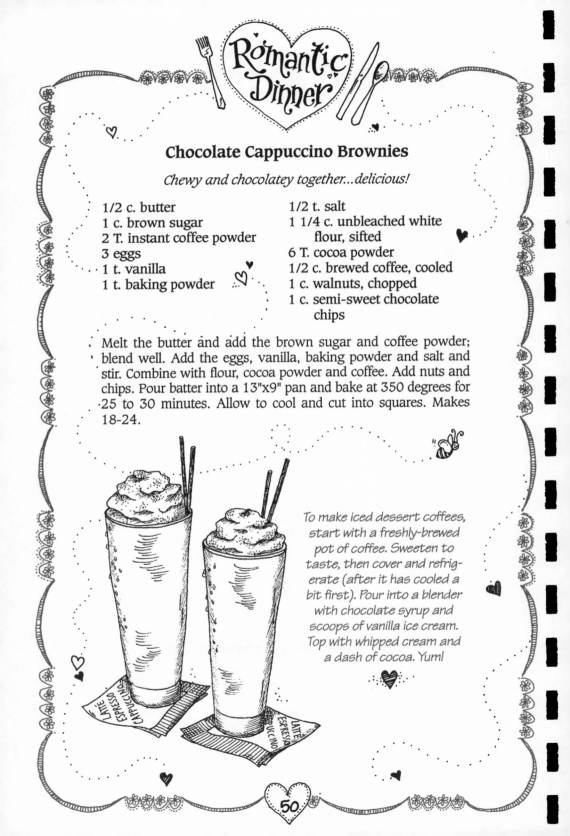

To make iced dessert coffees, start with a freshly-brewed pot of coffee. Sweeten to taste, then cover and refrigerate (after it has cooled a bit first). Pour into a blender with chocolate syrup and scoops of vanilla ice cream. Top with whipped cream and a dash of cocoa. Yum!

Special touches...

Floral Writing Papers

Make decorated placecards, notepapers or greeting cards with pressed flowers. First, press your flowers between sheets of blotting paper weighted down with heavy books. Allow the flowers to dry, then glue them to fancy notepaper available from stationery stores. For an added touch, use a felt-tipped calligraphy pen to write out your message.

Herbal Candle Ring

An easy craft idea for your tabletop. Start with a wreath base made of floral foam. Cover the base with Spanish moss, using floral pins to hold it in place. Attach floral picks to small bundles of dried sweet Annie and arrange the bunches around the wreath's inner and outer rims. Fill in the middle with more dried herbs and flowers. Choose from white and pink statice, larkspur, lavender, everlastings, oregano and roses. Spray the wreath with a commercial fixative. Place a pillar candle in the middle.

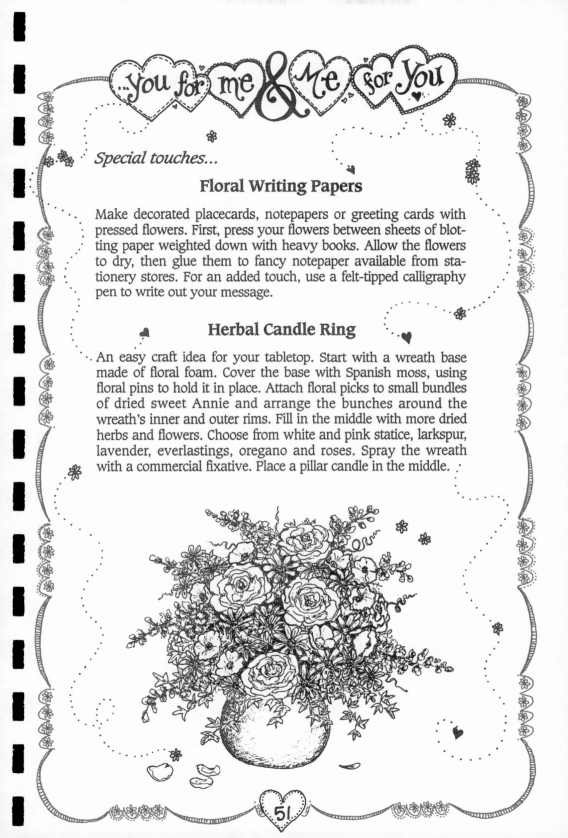

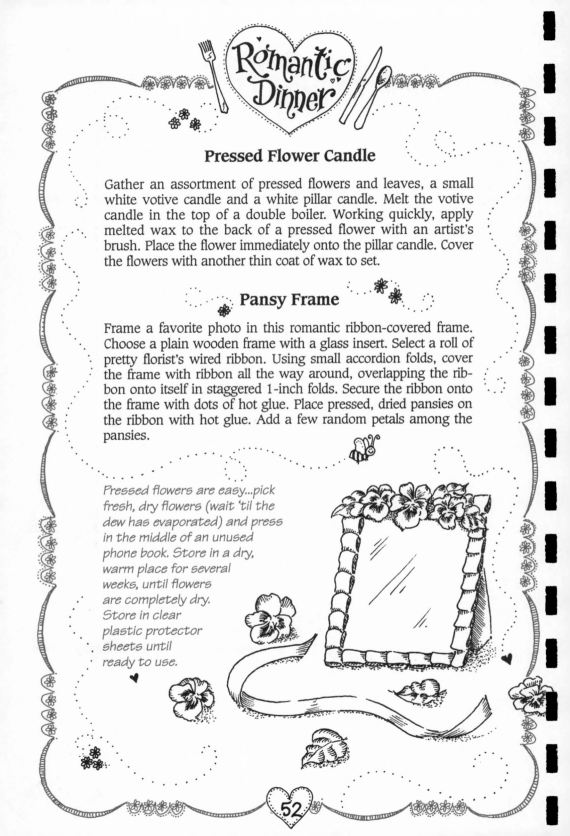

Romantic Dinner

Pressed Flower Candle

Gather an assortment of pressed flowers and leaves, a small white votive candle and a white pillar candle. Melt the votive candle in the top of a double boiler. Working quickly, apply melted wax to the back of a pressed flower with an artist's brush. Place the flower immediately onto the pillar candle. Cover the flowers with another thin coat of wax to set.

Pansy Frame

Frame a favorite photo in this romantic ribbon-covered frame. Choose a plain wooden frame with a glass insert. Select a roll of pretty florist's wired ribbon. Using small accordion folds, cover the frame with ribbon all the way around, overlapping the ribbon onto itself in staggered 1-inch folds. Secure the ribbon onto the frame with dots of hot glue. Place pressed, dried pansies on the ribbon with hot glue. Add a few random petals among the pansies.

Pressed flowers are easy...pick fresh, dry flowers (wait 'til the dew has evaporated) and press in the middle of an unused phone book. Store in a dry, warm place for several weeks, until flowers are completely dry. Store in clear plastic protector sheets until ready to use.

Afternoon Tea

...the pleasure of your company

Cucumber Sandwiches Dijon
Salmon and Cream Cheese Sandwiches
Walnut Tea Loaf
Lemon Cake
Orange Poppy Seed Bread
Honeydew Granité
Variety of Freshly Brewed Teas

A tea table without a big cake in the country in England would look very bare...the ideal table should include some sort of hot buttered toast or scone, one or two sorts of sandwiches, a plate of small light cakes and our friend the luncheon cake. Add a pot of jam or honey, and a plate of brown and white bread and butter...and every eye will sparkle, and all those wishing to follow the fashionable craze of slimming will groan in despair.

- Lady Sysonby, Lady Sysonby's Cookbook

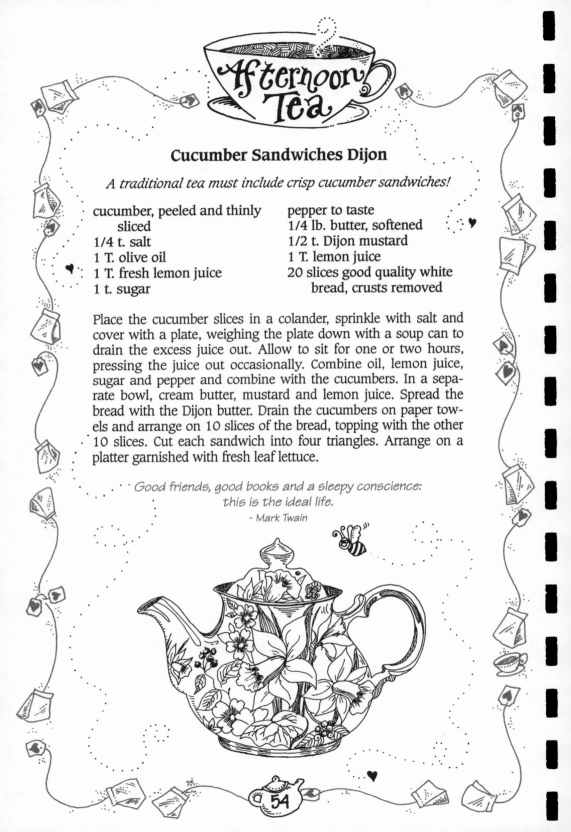

Afternoon Tea

Cucumber Sandwiches Dijon

A traditional tea must include crisp cucumber sandwiches!

cucumber, peeled and thinly
    sliced
1/4 t. salt
1 T. olive oil
1 T. fresh lemon juice
1 t. sugar

pepper to taste
1/4 lb. butter, softened
1/2 t. Dijon mustard
1 T. lemon juice
20 slices good quality white
    bread, crusts removed

Place the cucumber slices in a colander, sprinkle with salt and cover with a plate, weighing the plate down with a soup can to drain the excess juice out. Allow to sit for one or two hours, pressing the juice out occasionally. Combine oil, lemon juice, sugar and pepper and combine with the cucumbers. In a separate bowl, cream butter, mustard and lemon juice. Spread the bread with the Dijon butter. Drain the cucumbers on paper towels and arrange on 10 slices of the bread, topping with the other 10 slices. Cut each sandwich into four triangles. Arrange on a platter garnished with fresh leaf lettuce.

Good friends, good books and a sleepy conscience:
this is the ideal life.
- Mark Twain

the pleasure of your company

Walnut Tea Loaf

Not too sweet...moist and delicious.

1 1/3 c. honey
1 1/4 lb. butter, melted and
   cooled
2 eggs
1/2 c. whole milk
2 T. lemon juice

3 1/2 c. flour
3/4 t. baking soda
1/4 t. salt
1 t. ground cloves
1 c. walnuts, chopped
1/2 c. raisins (optional)

Combine honey, butter, eggs, milk and lemon juice until well blended. In a separate bowl, combine flour, baking soda, salt and cloves. Add flour mixture to the honey butter and beat until creamy. Fold in walnuts and raisins. Pour batter into two greased and floured 8 1/2"x4 1/2" loaf pans. Bake at 325 degrees for about one hour, or until a toothpick comes out clean. Cool for 15 minutes, then turn onto racks to cool completely.

*Afternoon tea is probably the simplest fashion
in which to exercise hospitality. Pretty cups and saucers
are among the possessions of which the young housekeeper
has a generous store, and they will make an attractive
array on her afternoon tea table.*
- Christine Terhune Herrick, 1902

Afternoon Tea

Salmon and Cream Cheese Sandwiches

For a colorful variation, add pimentos to the cream cheese mixture.

1/4 lb. smoked salmon, thinly sliced
4 oz. cream cheese, softened

1 T. fresh dill, minced, plus dill sprigs for garnish
8 slices pumpernickel bread

Combine salmon, cream cheese and dill. Remove crusts from bread and spread salmon mixture over bread slices. Cut each bread slice into fingers or squares and garnish with tiny sprigs of fresh dill.

If you approach each new person you meet in a spirit of adventure, you will find yourself endlessly fascinated by the new channels of thought and experience and personality that you encounter. I do not mean simply the famous people of the world, but people from every walk of life.

- Eleanor Roosevelt

♥ Lemon Cake

Arrange violets or daisies around this pretty bundt cake.

1/2 lb. sweet butter, softened
1 c. sugar
rind of 2 lemons, grated
1 T. lemon juice
1 c. sour cream

2 t. vanilla extract
6 egg whites
pinch of salt
2 c. flour
1 t. baking powder

Lemon-Butter Glaze:

3/4 c. powdered sugar
1/4 c. lemon juice
2 T. butter, melted

Cream butter with 1/2 cup sugar. Beat in lemon rind, juice, sour cream and vanilla. In a separate bowl, beat egg whites with salt until stiff. Gradually add remaining 1/2 cup of sugar to egg whites. In another bowl, mix flour and baking powder. Add dry ingredients to butter mixture, and 1/3 of the egg whites. Gradually add remaining egg whites, gently folding until mixed. Pour batter into a greased and floured bundt pan. Bake in a 350 degree oven for about 70 minutes, or until a toothpick comes out clean. Mix glaze ingredients together and drizzle over the cake after it has cooled.

What could be more perfect for a tea party than tea roses? Float tea rose blossoms in shallow glass bowls filled with water, or arrange them in single-color or mixed bouquets all around the house.

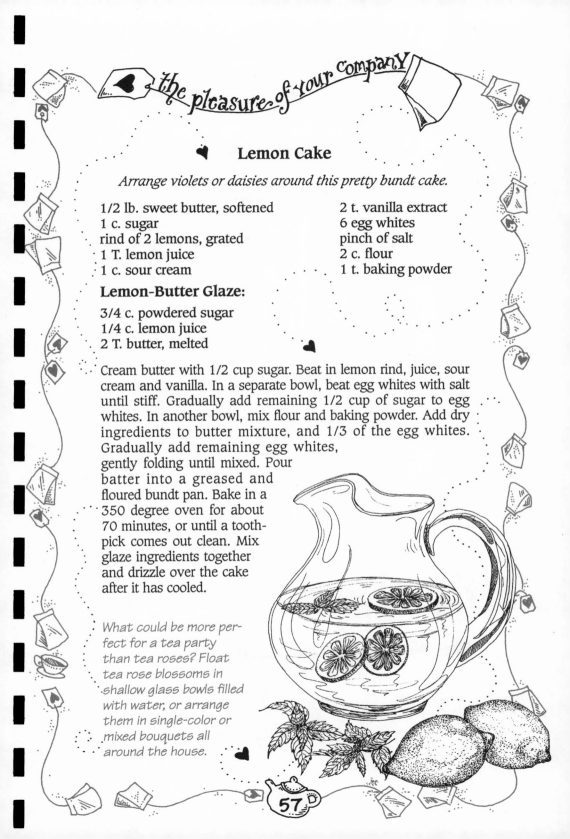

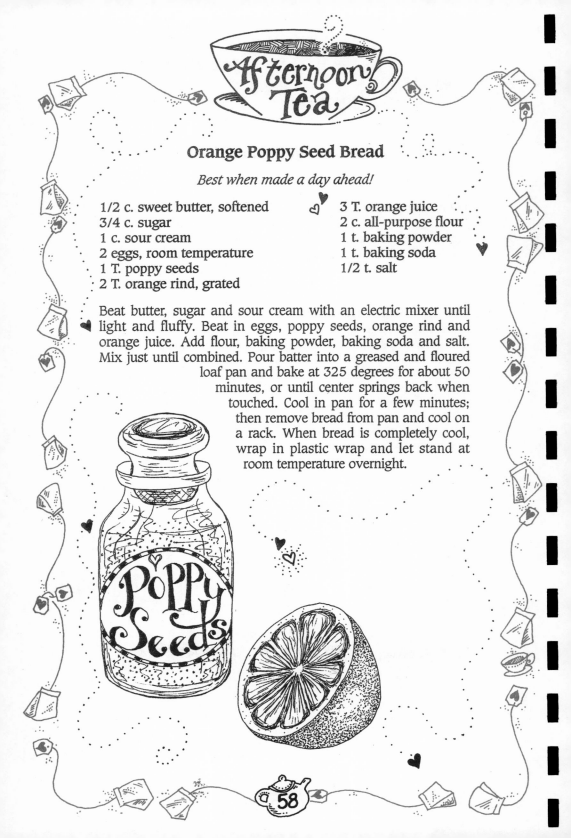

Afternoon Tea

Orange Poppy Seed Bread

Best when made a day ahead!

1/2 c. sweet butter, softened	3 T. orange juice
3/4 c. sugar	2 c. all-purpose flour
1 c. sour cream	1 t. baking powder
2 eggs, room temperature	1 t. baking soda
1 T. poppy seeds	1/2 t. salt
2 T. orange rind, grated	

Beat butter, sugar and sour cream with an electric mixer until light and fluffy. Beat in eggs, poppy seeds, orange rind and orange juice. Add flour, baking powder, baking soda and salt. Mix just until combined. Pour batter into a greased and floured loaf pan and bake at 325 degrees for about 50 minutes, or until center springs back when touched. Cool in pan for a few minutes; then remove bread from pan and cool on a rack. When bread is completely cool, wrap in plastic wrap and let stand at room temperature overnight.

Poppy Seeds

Honeydew Granité

A refreshing end to the perfect tea.

1/2 c. sugar	6 T. fresh lemon juice
1/2 c. water	4 T. vodka
1 ripe honeydew melon, peeled, seeded and cubed	1/2 t. freshly ground pepper

Combine sugar and water in a saucepan and bring to a boil over medium heat. Reduce heat and simmer for 5 minutes. Set aside until cool. Process melon in a blender along with the sugar syrup and lemon juice until smooth. Add vodka and pepper and blend well. Pour into a large glass or pottery pie plate and place in the freezer. Stir every half hour or so until frozen. To serve, use a large spoon to scrape the granité into serving dishes. Serves 8.

How to pick a melon? A melon should feel nice and heavy and dense...heavier than it appears...and should have no scar at the stem indicating it was picked prematurely.

Time for Tea

Afternoon Tea

Freshly Brewed Teas

Here are some guidelines for perfect pots of tea...

- Be sure to use cold, rather than warm water. Cold water is fresh and full of oxygen.
- If you're filling tea balls with loose tea, leave some space for the tea leaves to expand as they steep.
- Select good quality teas.
- Better to make the tea too strong than too weak, as strong tea can always be diluted.
- Use a pottery, ceramic or silver pot, but not an aluminum or enamel-coated metal for best flavor.
- As soon as the kettle of water boils, remove it from the heat immediately and pour it into the teapot. Continued boiling will spoil the taste of the tea.

There are few hours in life more agreeable than the hours dedicated to the ceremony known as afternoon tea.
- Henry James

Some Types of Fine Teas

Darjeeling - Known to be one of the finest teas in the world, it grows near Nepal, high in the mountains. Tastes of black currant.

Earl Grey - A blend of black teas which have been crushed and fermented before drying. Tastes of bergamot, an Italian citrus fruit.

English Breakfast - From India, a blend of strong teas blended for a brisk morning wake-up.

Oolong - From Taiwan, it has a peachy flavor that is almost irresistible.

Gunpowder - Grown in China, this green tea is picked and rolled, leaf by leaf, into tight rolls. A very delicate flavor.

Jasmine - Usually a mix of black and green tea with jasmine flowers added for flavor.

Lapsang Souchong - A rich, hearty tea from China.

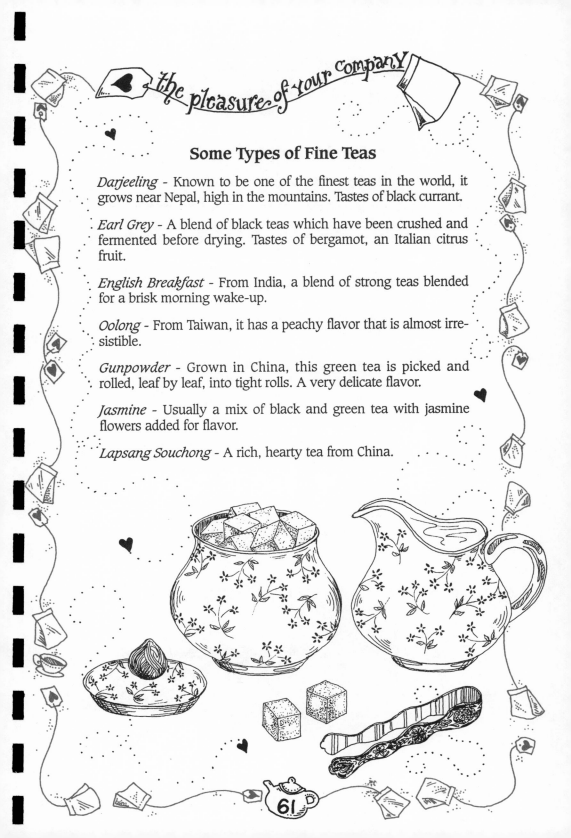

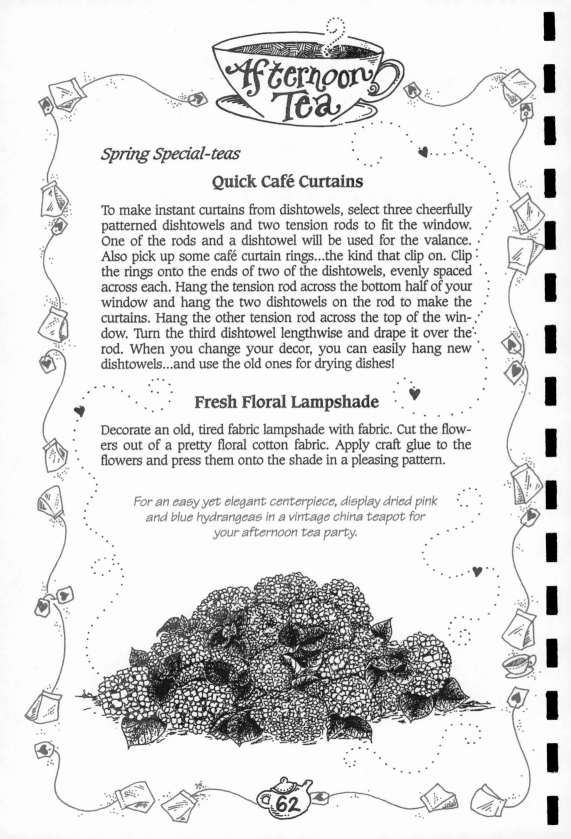

Afternoon Tea

Spring Special-teas

Quick Café Curtains

To make instant curtains from dishtowels, select three cheerfully patterned dishtowels and two tension rods to fit the window. One of the rods and a dishtowel will be used for the valance. Also pick up some café curtain rings...the kind that clip on. Clip the rings onto the ends of two of the dishtowels, evenly spaced across each. Hang the tension rod across the bottom half of your window and hang the two dishtowels on the rod to make the curtains. Hang the other tension rod across the top of the window. Turn the third dishtowel lengthwise and drape it over the rod. When you change your decor, you can easily hang new dishtowels...and use the old ones for drying dishes!

Fresh Floral Lampshade

Decorate an old, tired fabric lampshade with fabric. Cut the flowers out of a pretty floral cotton fabric. Apply craft glue to the flowers and press them onto the shade in a pleasing pattern.

For an easy yet elegant centerpiece, display dried pink and blue hydrangeas in a vintage china teapot for your afternoon tea party.

Sugar Cookie Cups

Make your favorite sugar cookie recipe, cutting the cookies into 5" rounds. Remove the cookies from the oven a bit early, while they're still soft, and press them into custard cups. Fill with pudding or fresh berries and top with whipped cream.

♥ Lemon Pomander Ball

Pierce several lemons all over with an icepick in an evenly-spaced spiral pattern. Insert whole cloves into the lemons and sprinkle with cinnamon. Arrange the lemons in a pottery bowl or basket and use as a fresh-smelling decoration for your kitchen counter or breakfast table.

Lemons will keep 3 to 4 days at room temperature. You can keep fresh lemons up to a month in the refrigerator in a sealed plastic bag.

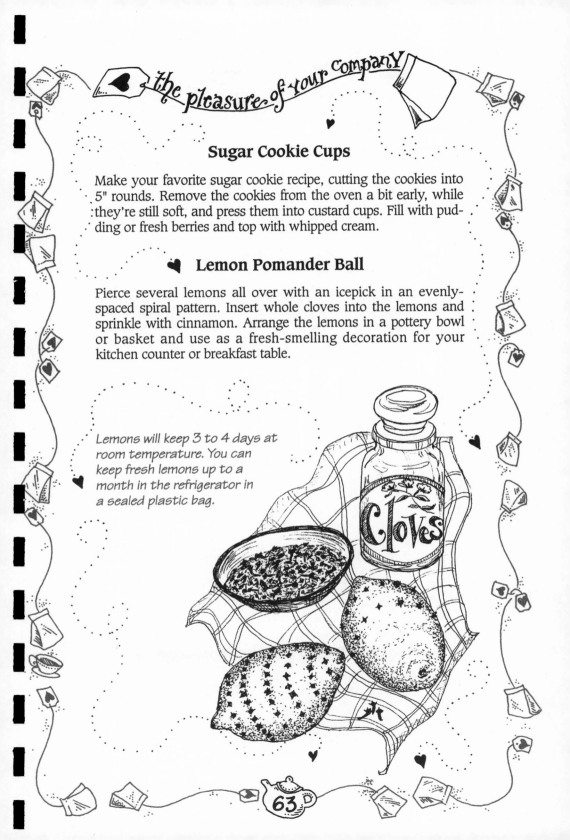

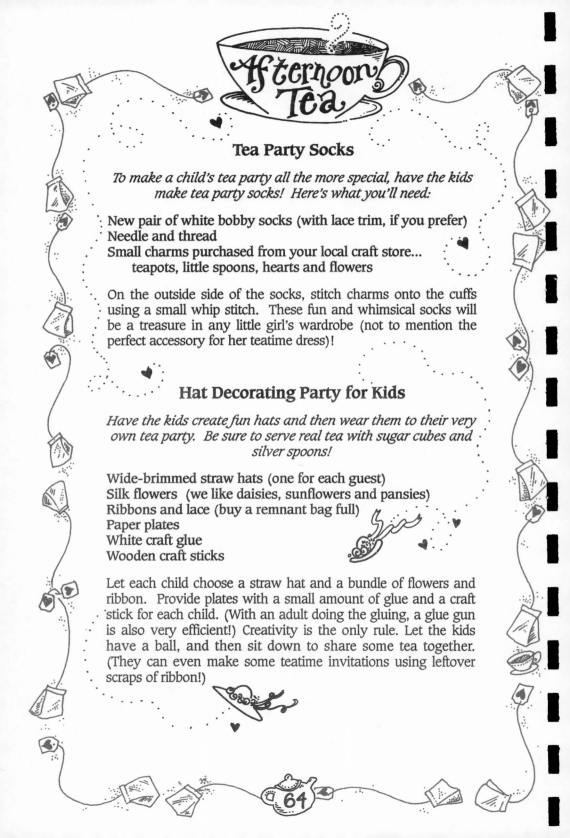

Afternoon Tea

Tea Party Socks

To make a child's tea party all the more special, have the kids make tea party socks! Here's what you'll need:

New pair of white bobby socks (with lace trim, if you prefer)
Needle and thread
Small charms purchased from your local craft store...
   teapots, little spoons, hearts and flowers

On the outside side of the socks, stitch charms onto the cuffs using a small whip stitch. These fun and whimsical socks will be a treasure in any little girl's wardrobe (not to mention the perfect accessory for her teatime dress)!

Hat Decorating Party for Kids

Have the kids create fun hats and then wear them to their very own tea party. Be sure to serve real tea with sugar cubes and silver spoons!

Wide-brimmed straw hats (one for each guest)
Silk flowers (we like daisies, sunflowers and pansies)
Ribbons and lace (buy a remnant bag full)
Paper plates
White craft glue
Wooden craft sticks

Let each child choose a straw hat and a bundle of flowers and ribbon. Provide plates with a small amount of glue and a craft stick for each child. (With an adult doing the gluing, a glue gun is also very efficient!) Creativity is the only rule. Let the kids have a ball, and then sit down to share some tea together. (They can even make some teatime invitations using leftover scraps of ribbon!)

Country Wedding
...elegant outdoor feast

Smoked Salmon Cones with Horseradish Cream
Pinwheel Sandwiches
Curried Chicken Salad
Cheese-Walnut Grape Rounds
Roquefort Cut-out Crackers
Ladyfingers
Fudge-Topped Cherry Hearts
Blushing Pink Punch Bowl

Come live with me, and be my love,
And we will some new pleasures prove
Of golden sands, and crystal brooks,
With silken lines, and silver hooks.
- John Donne

Smoked Salmon Cones with Horseradish Cream

These appetizers can be prepared ahead and refrigerated for up to 3 hours.

6 slices brown bread, thinly
    sliced
1/2 c. heavy cream

2 T. horseradish
10 oz. smoked salmon, very
    thinly sliced into 2"
    squares

Trim crusts off bread and cut each slice into four squares. Wrap in plastic and set aside. Beat cream until smooth and stiff peaks form; add horseradish. To assemble, roll salmon squares into cone shapes and place on bread squares. Using a pastry bag, fill each salmon cone with horseradish cream.

Pinwheel Sandwiches

Cover these appetizers with moistened lettuce leaves to prevent drying out before serving.

6 slices soft white bread, thinly sliced
3/4 c. sandwich filling

Roll out bread slices with a rolling pin until flat. Spread slices with your favorite filling (some of our favorites: crab salad with dill and tuna salad with rosemary.) Spread side up, roll each slice into long rolls. When ready to serve, slice the rolls into half-inch slices and arrange pinwheels on appetizer tray.

Curried Chicken Salad

The pineapple and curry add that gourmet touch.

2 c. cooked boneless chicken
   breasts, diced
1 apple, peeled and cubed
1 c. fresh pineapple, diced
1/4 c. golden raisins

1/3 c. dates, chopped
2 T. chutney, chopped
1/2 t. salt

Dressing:

2 t. curry powder
2 T. chicken broth

1 c. mayonnaise

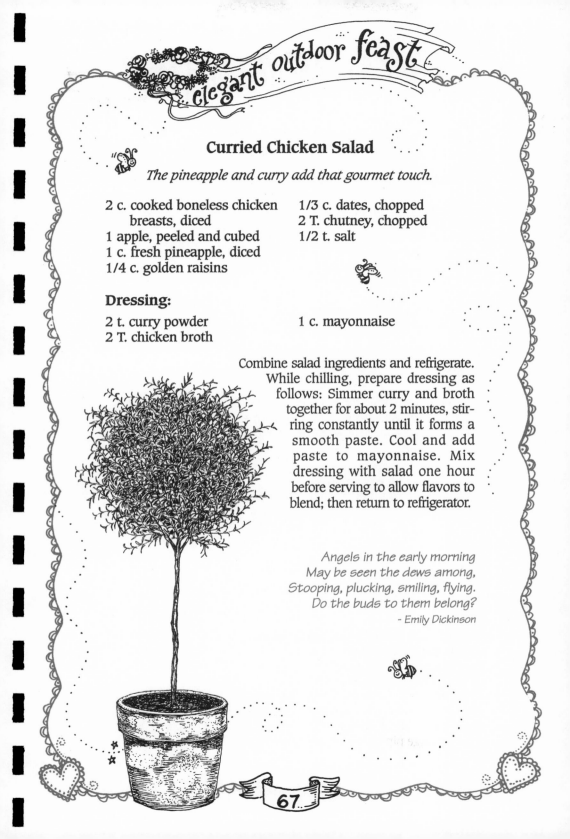

Combine salad ingredients and refrigerate. While chilling, prepare dressing as follows: Simmer curry and broth together for about 2 minutes, stirring constantly until it forms a smooth paste. Cool and add paste to mayonnaise. Mix dressing with salad one hour before serving to allow flavors to blend; then return to refrigerator.

*Angels in the early morning
May be seen the dews among,
Stooping, plucking, smiling, flying.
Do the buds to them belong?*
- Emily Dickinson

Cheese-Walnut Grape Rounds

The grapes are a nice surprise inside the cheese. Try green olives for a different taste.

8 oz. pkg. cream cheese, softened
8 oz. pkg. sharp cheddar cheese, grated
1/2 c. butter, softened
1 T. Dijon mustard
1/2 t. Worcestershire sauce
large bunch seedless grapes
2 T. paprika
3/4 c. walnuts, chopped

Beat together cheeses, butter, mustard and Worcestershire sauce. With damp hands, form cheese mixture around individual grapes. Roll each grape in paprika, then in chopped nuts, and chill until set. Makes approximately 50 appetizers.

As a wedding keepsake, decorate an unfinished blanket chest with stain or antiquing; then stencil on the names of the happy couple along with their wedding date. Cover with two coats of clear varnish.

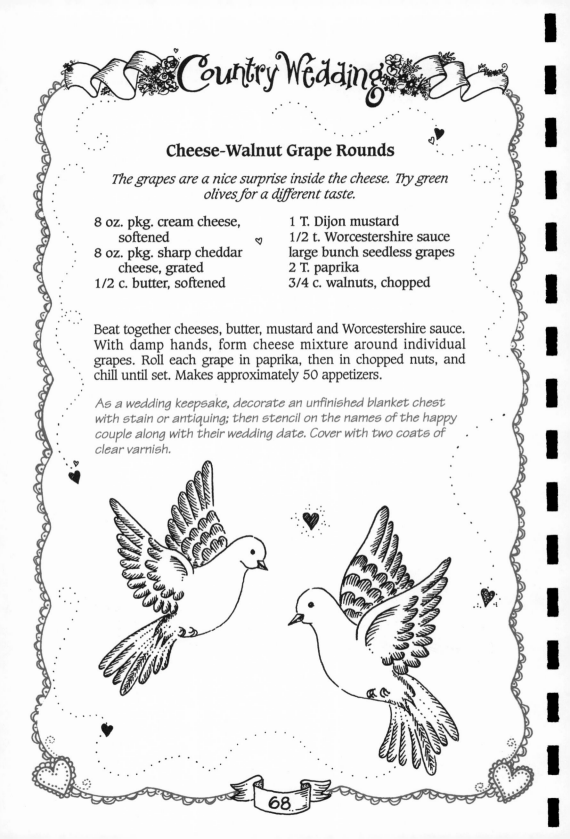

Roquefort Cut-out Crackers

Delicate cheese wafers with a touch of hot pepper!

1 c. flour, preferably unbleached
7 T. Roquefort cheese crumbles
1 large egg yolk
4 t. heavy cream

7 T. butter, softened
pinch of salt
cayenne pepper to taste
1/2 t. dried parsley

Mix all ingredients together and roll into a dough. Let rest for half an hour, then roll dough out to about 1/8" thick. Use your favorite spring shapes (flowers, teacups, wedding bells) to cut out the crackers. Bake on an ungreased cookie sheet at 400 degrees for 8 to 10 minutes. Be sure to keep an eye on them. Remove the delicate crackers carefully when cool.

Along with the fancy hors d'oeuvres, set out pretty bowls of salty toasted nuts, flavorful olives, caviar, dried figs and apricots, salsas and chips, veggies and dips, pesto and bread rounds.

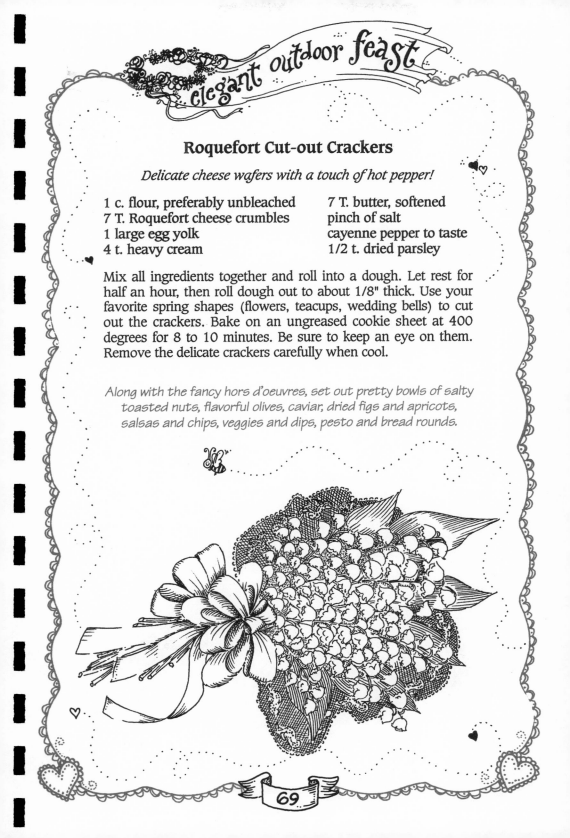

Ladyfingers

Delicate and delicious with coffee or tea.

3 eggs, separated
pinch of salt
1/8 t. cream of tartar
1/2 c. sugar, divided
1 t. vanilla

pinch of nutmeg, grated
1/8 t. almond extract
scant 1/2 c. flour
2 T. cornstarch
1/2 c. powdered sugar, sifted

Beat three egg whites until foamy. Add the salt and cream of tartar and beat again until soft peaks are formed. Beat in 1/4 cup of the sugar a spoonful at a time. Continue to beat for one minute on high speed. In a separate bowl, beat the egg yolks and add vanilla, nutmeg, almond extract and the remaining 1/4 cup of sugar. Beat well until light in color. Pour over egg whites and fold together. Sift flour and cornstarch together and sprinkle gradually over the egg mixture. Fold in very gently with a spatula, so mixture is very light. Transfer half the batter into a pastry bag with a 3/4-inch plain tip. Pipe the batter onto a large greased cookie sheet. Make the ladyfingers about 1 1/2 inches wide and 4 inches long. Dust with the powdered sugar. Bake 20 minutes at 300 degrees, until golden. Turn heat off and leave ladyfingers in the oven for another 5 minutes. Remove from sheet and cool on rack.

A bleached heart-shaped basket makes a beautiful centerpiece. Fill with white violets, roses and baby's breath.

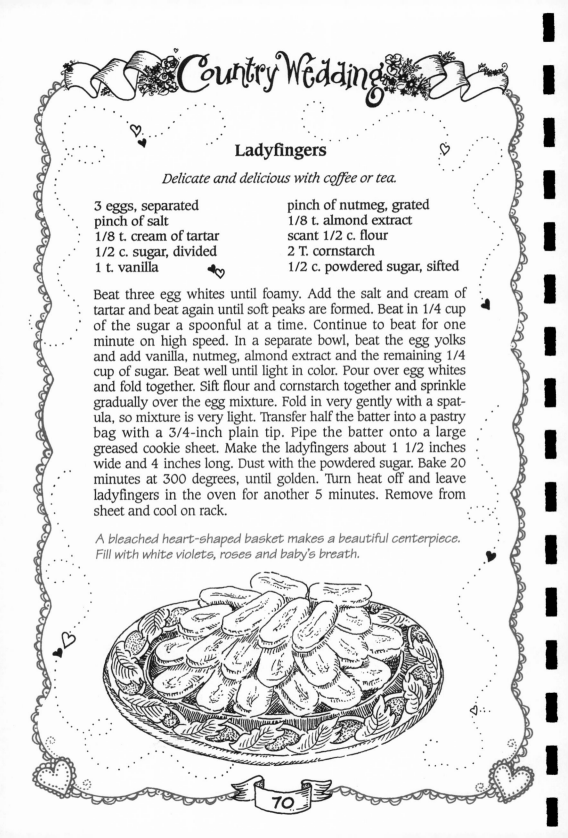

Fudge-Topped Cherry Hearts

Prepared ingredients make these quick and easy to make!

8 oz. pkg. frozen puff pastry
    sheets, thawed
3/4 c. cherry pie filling

8 t. fudge sauce (ice cream
    topping)
2 T. almonds, chopped

Preheat oven to 375 degrees. Unfold pastry onto lightly floured surface. Using a heart-shaped cookie cutter, cut pastry into 8 hearts. Place hearts onto ungreased cookie sheet and bake for 15 to 18 minutes until golden. Cool and split hearts horizontally. Spoon cherry pie filling inside each heart and replace tops. To serve, heat fudge sauce until smooth and drizzle over hearts. Sprinkle with nuts and serve immediately. Serves 8.

*Love is an irresistible desire to
be irresistibly desired.*
- Robert Frost

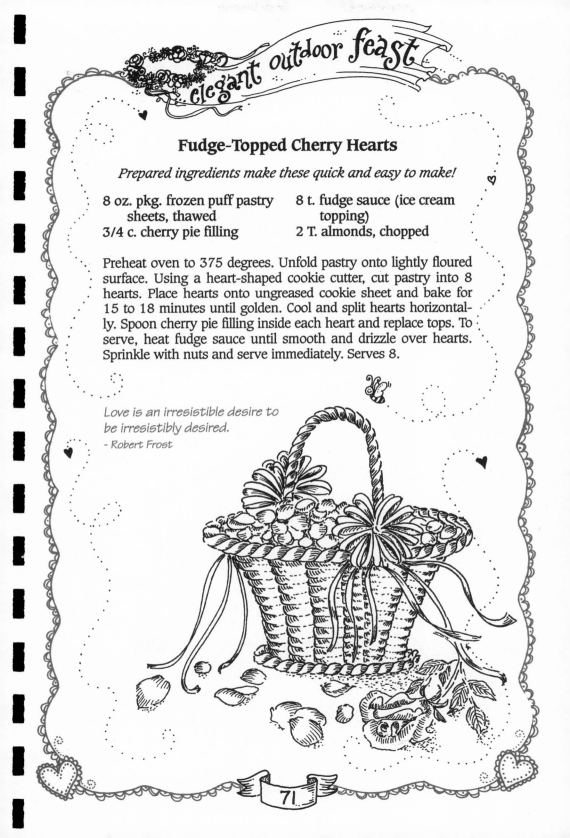

Blushing Pink Punch Bowl

Float pink and white rose petals and slices of lime on top.

2 c. hibiscus tea	1 gallon rosé wine
2 qts. water	2 qts. sparkling water
1 1/2 c. honey	1 lime, sliced

Tie the loose tea into a cheesecloth bag and drop in boiling water. Steep, covered, about 10 minutes. Remove tea bag and add honey, stirring to dissolve. Cool completely and pour into a gallon container. Add sparkling water and stir. To serve, mix tea with the wine in a punch bowl over ice and add rose petals and lime as garnish. Makes 2 gallons.

Wedding veils were originally designed to protect the bride from evil spirits. The custom of throwing the veil back after the ceremony was to ensure the groom had the right bride! (Seems a little late, doesn't it?)

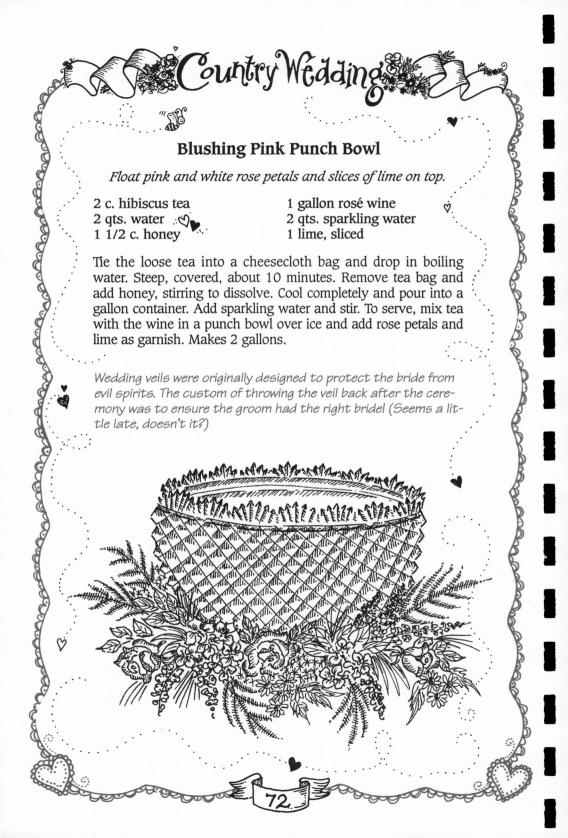

Beautiful Cakes

A wedding cake can be as individual as you are. Used to be, wedding cakes were white with fluffy white frosting and a little bride and groom on top. Today, you can select your favorite flavor, whether it be chocolate-raspberry, carrot, spice, almond, mocha, orange or lemon. You can decorate the top of the cake with fresh flowers, berries, lemon leaves, satin ribbons, chocolate curls, white chocolate molded flowers or baby's breath. Many couples today are incorporating hobbies and interests into their cakes...for example, instead of a bride and groom on top, they may have a little pair of tennis racquets, skis and poles, miniature gardening tools or any symbol that is most significant to them. Display your cake on a beautiful silver platter, in a large square basket, on a big bread board or a fabric-covered heart. You can decorate the base of your cake with fresh flowers and greenery to match your bridal bouquet.

Dainty little maiden, whither
would you wander?
Whither from this pretty
home, the home where
mother dwells?
'Far and far away,' said
the dainty little maiden,
'All among the gardens,
auriculas, anemones,
Roses and lilies and
Canterbury-bells.'
- Alfred Lord Tennyson

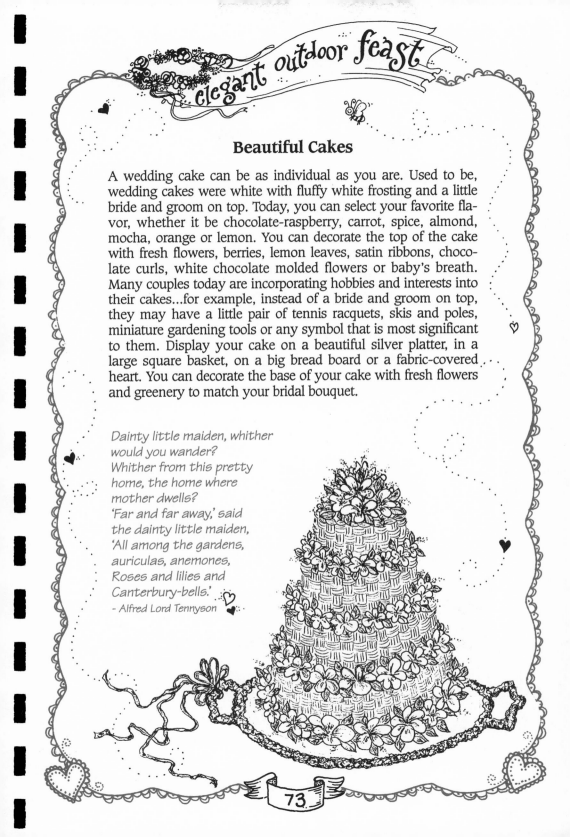

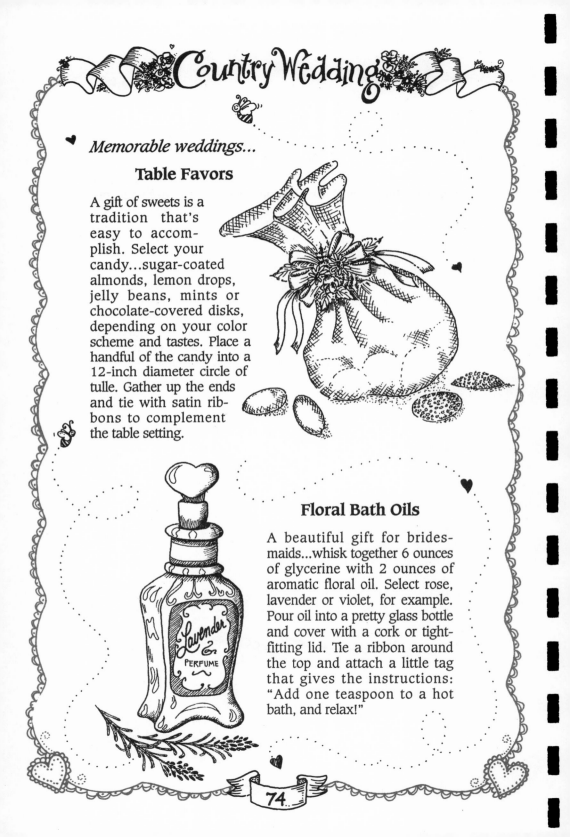

Country Wedding

Memorable weddings...

Table Favors

A gift of sweets is a tradition that's easy to accomplish. Select your candy...sugar-coated almonds, lemon drops, jelly beans, mints or chocolate-covered disks, depending on your color scheme and tastes. Place a handful of the candy into a 12-inch diameter circle of tulle. Gather up the ends and tie with satin ribbons to complement the table setting.

Floral Bath Oils

A beautiful gift for bridesmaids...whisk together 6 ounces of glycerine with 2 ounces of aromatic floral oil. Select rose, lavender or violet, for example. Pour oil into a pretty glass bottle and cover with a cork or tight-fitting lid. Tie a ribbon around the top and attach a little tag that gives the instructions: "Add one teaspoon to a hot bath, and relax!"

Lacy Ring Pillow

It's so easy to make a fancy little ring pillow out of lacy hand-kerchiefs! Simply stitch two hankies together and stuff with cotton batting; then sew up the remaining side. Add a wide ribbon trim all around the edge...choose white or a coordinating color. Attach a little ribbon loop to the middle, fastened with hook and loop fabric, for keeping the ring safe and sound.

Framed Invitation

Set the invitation on a standard-sized piece of matboard with enough margin to add border items. Save and press some of the flowers from the centerpiece, bits of ribbon, lace, and a small photo of the bride and groom. Surround the invitation with these items and glue into place, then insert into a ready-made frame.

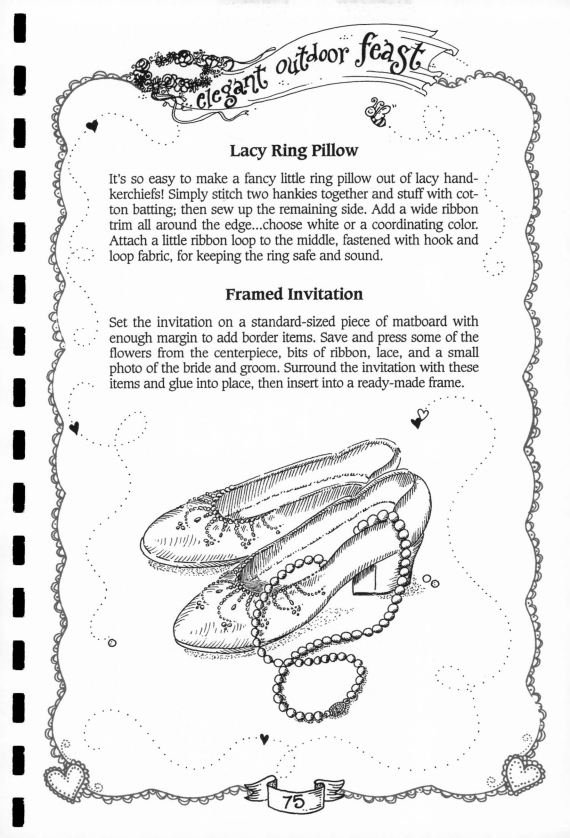

Sponge-Painted Pots

Giant terra cotta pots look beautiful at a country wedding. You can sponge-paint them in white, mustard or any combination of your wedding colors. Fill the pots with impatiens, geraniums, black-eyed Susans or your flowers of choice. Wrap wide wired ribbons around the pots and make huge bows. Line the pots up at the entrance, flank the buffet tables...the ideas are endless!

Table Decorating Ideas

For a country wedding, cover your buffet table in antique lace. You can use a coordinating color underneath for a gentle hint of color. Fill a large gathering basket with Queen Anne's lace, violets, white cosmos and black-eyed Susans. If your wedding party will extend into nighttime, be sure to place lots of white pillar candles in sparkling glass containers...canning jars, jelly jars, brandy snifters and hurricane lamps. Keep bugs away with citronella candles attached to garden stakes and planted all around the area.

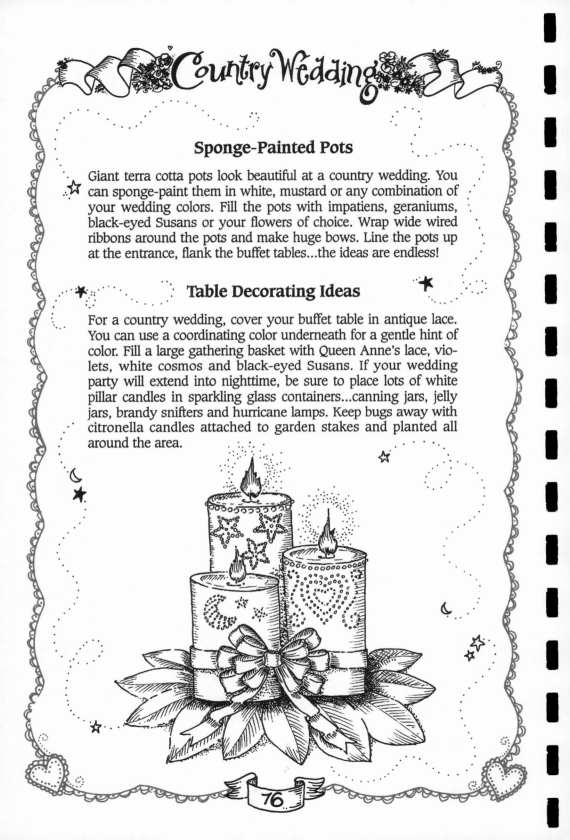

April Showers

...rainy day delights

Chicken Soup with Pasta and Tomatoes
Dilly Cheese Bread
Fresh Rhubarb Pie
Rainy Day Cupboard
Fragrant Kitchen Garland
Just for You

The sun was warm but the wind was chill.
You know how it is with an April day
When the sun is out and wind is still,
You're one month on in the middle of May.
But if you so much as dare to speak,
A cloud comes over the sunlit arch,
A wind comes off a frozen peak,
And you're two months back in the middle of March.
- Robert Frost

April Showers

Chicken Soup with Pasta and Tomatoes

*What could taste better than chicken soup on
a rainy spring day?*

1 T. olive oil
2 garlic cloves, peeled and
    crushed
1 1/2 t. dried basil, crumbled
1/2 t. dried tarragon,
    crumbled
1 c. Italian plum tomatoes,
    chopped
1/4 c. chopped fresh parsley,
    plus more for garnish

2 T. tomato paste
5 c. low-salt chicken broth
1 c. dry white wine
3 large boneless, skinless
    chicken breasts, chopped
8 large oil-packed sun-dried
    tomatoes, sliced
1 c. penne pasta, cooked
    al dente
Parmesan or Romano cheese,
    freshly grated

In a large heavy pot over medium heat, combine the oil, garlic,
basil and tarragon and sauté about one minute. Mix in tomatoes, parsley, tomato paste, broth and wine and bring to a simmer. Add chicken and sun-dried tomatoes, cover pot and cook
about 15 minutes, or until chicken is cooked through. Add pasta
and cook until just heated
through. Season with salt
and pepper if
desired. Garnish
with parsley
and cheese.

Dilly Cheese Bread

Tasty bread will add some sunshine to a chilly gray day.

3/4 c. milk
1 1/2 T. dill seeds, chopped
1 T. honey
1/4 c. vegetable oil
3 eggs, room temperature,
   blended

2 1/2 c. whole wheat flour
1 pkg. dry yeast
1 1/2 t. salt
3 1/2 c. packed sharp
   cheddar cheese, grated
3 T. fresh dill, chopped

Bring milk, dill seeds and honey to a simmer in a small saucepan; allow to cool until just warm. Whisk in oil and eggs. In a separate bowl, combine 1 1/4 cup flour, yeast, salt and 2 cups of the cheese. Add warm milk mixture and fresh dill and beat with electric mixer for 3 minutes. Add remaining flour and beat 2 more minutes. Cover bowl with plastic and let the dough rise in a warm area about 75 minutes, or until doubled in size. Spoon half of batter in a greased 9"x5" loaf pan. Sprinkle remaining cheese over batter. Cover with remaining batter and smooth the top. (Do not force the batter down.) Cover and allow to rise another 30 minutes. Bake in a 350 degree oven about 45 minutes, or until bread is golden and makes a hollow sound when tapped.

April Showers

Fresh Rhubarb Pie

Use prepared pastry and freshly-picked rhubarb.
You'll love this pie!

2 eggs
1 c. sour cream
1 1/2 c. sugar
2 T. flour
1 t. vanilla
1/4 t. salt

3 c. fresh rhubarb, chopped
prepared pie crust for single-
   crust pie
1/4 c. light brown sugar, packed
1/4 c. flour
3 T. butter

Mix together eggs, sour cream, sugar, 2 tablespoons flour, vanilla, and salt. Add rhubarb. Fill the prepared crust with this mixture and cover crust with foil. Bake in a 450 oven for 15 minutes; reduce temperature to 350 degrees and bake 20-25 minutes longer. While pie is baking, mix the brown sugar and 1/4
cup flour. Add butter and mash
with a fork until mixture is
crumbly. Sprinkle over pie.
Bake the pie uncovered 20
minutes longer, until set.

On a rainy day, sort
through your button box
and select the bright-
est, cheeriest buttons.
Glue several onto a large
pin back and allow to dry
overnight. A great way
to perk up a casual
denim shirt.

rainy day Delights

Rainy Day Cupboard

Keep certain games and projects special by saving them especially for rainy days. Fill your "Rainy Day Cupboard" with all the ingredients to keep your kids busy, happy and creative.

crayons, paints, markers and colored pencils
construction paper
blank sketch books
pipe cleaners
string
cardboard
wooden sticks from frozen treats
egg cartons
glue stick, white glue and tape

glitter
scraps of fabric, lace, ribbons and felt
stapler
stickers
scissors, pinking shears, safety scissors
magazines and used cards for cut-outs
wallpaper books

Be sure to display finished projects in a scrapbook or on the fridge. Some creations even deserve framing. You'll treasure them over the years!

Fragrant Kitchen Garland

A lovely gift idea.

You will need:

electric drill with small bit	cinnamon sticks
wire cutters	walnut shells
5-2"x12" rag strips in	dried apple slices
kitchen colors	dried orange slices
whole bay leaves	60" of 20 gauge spool wire
whole nutmegs	(plastic coated is best)

Drill tiny holes through the nutmegs, cinnamon sticks and walnut shells. Using the wire cutters, make a point on one end of the spool wire. Leave the wire on the spool while you string the leaves, spices, shells and fruit slices in a pleasing repetitive order. For example, you may want to string 10 bay leaves, 3 nutmegs, 5 cinnamon sticks, 3 walnut shells, 2 apple slices and 2 orange slices. Tie five rag bows or strips onto the garland. When you are finished, make a loop at each end of the wire and twist the ends securely onto the length of the wire. Use the loops to hang the garland over a windowsill or doorway.

Dry fruit slices in the sun using an herb drying screen or a clean window screen.

Just for You...

We all need a little time and space devoted to our own well-being. We can give so much more to others when we've given to ourselves. Here are a few "gifts" you can bestow on yourself.

Homemade Bread

Indulge yourself in the most wonderful aroma in the world...that of freshly-baked yeast-rising bread. You may find that the whole process of kneading, punching, and watching it turn golden in the oven is very therapeutic...and so is eating a warm, fresh slice, spread with sweet soft butter. Or, if you want the benefits without the work, purchase frozen bread dough and pop it in the oven. You'll still get that comforting aroma that has stirred memories of home for generations on end! Here's one of our favorite bread recipes...

Oatmeal Bread

3 c. oatmeal	1/4 c. butter
1 T. salt	1/3 c. lukewarm water
1/3 c. + 2 T. honey	2 T. yeast
1 3/4 c. heavy cream	2 c. unbleached white flour

Preheat oven to 375 degrees. Combine oatmeal, salt and 1/3 cup honey in a large bowl. In a saucepan, heat cream, butter and water until butter is melted. Pour butter mixture over the oatmeal mixture and allow to stand until just lukewarm. In a separate bowl, combine the water, yeast and 2 tablespoons honey and allow to sit while oatmeal is cooling. When yeast is bubbling, combine the yeast-honey mixture with the oatmeal mixture and gradually add flour until dough is stiff. Knead for about 5 minutes on a floured breadboard, until dough is smooth. Grease a bowl and place dough in it to rise for about an hour, or until it has doubled. Punch down the dough and separate it into three medium-sized loaves. Place into greased bread pans and let rise again for about 45 minutes. Bake for 40 to 45 minutes, or until the crust sounds hollow when thumped with your finger.

Personal Journal

Sometimes the demands of day-to-day living cause us to lose contact with our innermost thoughts and feelings. As a way of keeping in touch with yourself, consider recording your thoughts, dreams and inspirations in a journal. Blank books are widely available in bookstores and stationery shops, some with elaborate and beautiful covers. Or, you can cover a regular notebook with fabric and glue, making the design your very own. Along with your thoughts, you can press flowers, paste in theater tickets, save special photographs. Keep a good-quality pen with your journal to encourage frequent writing. Journal-writing is very satisfying in itself, and who knows? It may lead to an interesting biography one day!

The grass has so little to do,
A sphere of simple green,
With only butterflies to brood,
And bees to entertain.
-Emily Dickinson

Lavender Pillow Sachets

Lavender lifts the spirits. You can grow your own lavender or purchase everything you need in an herb or craft shop.

2 c. dried lavender leaves
1/2 c. dried cornflowers
1 1/2 t. orris root powder
1 1/2 c. dried lavender buds

3/4 c. dried juniper berries
8 drops lavender oil
4 drops rosemary oil
several 4" squares of fabric,
    needle and thread

Combine all ingredients (except fabric, needle and thread) in a glazed pottery bowl and cover tightly. Allow fragrances to blend and mellow for at least two weeks. Select muslin, calico or homespun fabrics of your choice. Handstitch or sew three edges of two squares fitted together. Fill pouches with potpourri and sew remaining seams closed. Tuck these little "pillows" wherever you need a lift...inside your pillowcase, in your sweater drawer, in the linen closet. Make them as fancy as you wish with ribbon roses, lace and appliqués. Make enough to give as gifts, or fill a pretty basket.

Tie your linens with a sachet-adorned ribbon and tuck in a fresh sprig of lavender to make them smell and look fresh and beautiful.

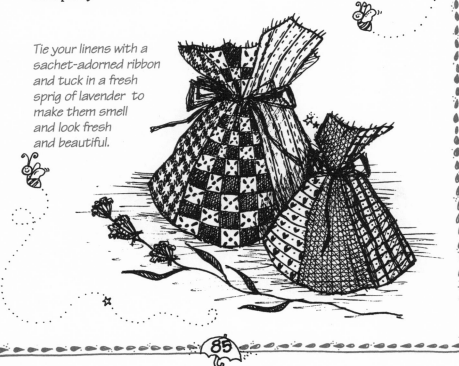

Fragrant Massage Oil

Relieve aching muscles with essential oils.

1/2 oz. olive oil	8 drops lavender oil
3 drops chamomile oil	3 drops ginger oil
3 drops birch oil	3 drops rosemary oil

Combine all oils and massage into tense muscles after a warm bath.

Treat yourself to an adventure. Do something you've never done before! Visit a new town and explore the shops...take dancing or swimming or painting lessons...go mushroom-hunting...go on a retreat. An adventure can renew your spirits and awaken your senses. You'll feel refreshed and vibrant.

May Day Bouquet

Lift someone else's spirits, and yours will be lifted as well. This pretty little May Day bouquet will give someone a welcome lift when you hang it on their doorknob. Dip a crocheted doily into fabric stiffener and ring out slightly. Mold the doily around a bundle of dried flowers and tie around the middle with satin ribbons. Loop any extra-long ribbons at the top for hanging. Let doily air dry for at least 24 hours and your bouquet is ready to give.

The rain is raining all around,
It falls on field and tree,
It rains on the umbrellas here,
And on the ships at sea.
-Robert Louis Stevenson

Especially for Mom

...treats a mother could love

Easy Red Potato Frittata
Sautéed Tomatoes with Tarragon
Herbal Omelet
Orange Muffins
Strawberry Spinach Salad
Mother's Luscious Chocolate Cake
Almond Tea

She mixes blue and mauve and green,
Purple and orange, white and red,
And all the colors in between
To patch a cover for her bed.

...And then across the bed it lies,
A thing of gorgeous crazy bloom,
As if a rainbow in the skies
Had shattered in her little room.
- Elizabeth Fleming

Easy Red Potato Frittata

*Mom will love this for breakfast with a toasted English muffin
and fresh berries on the side.*

3 egg whites
1 egg
2 T. chives, chopped
1/8 t. salt
1/8 t. pepper, freshly ground

1/2 c. baby red potatoes,
    diced
1/4 c. red pepper, chopped
1/2 broccoli flowerets
1/3 c. water
1/2 t. vegetable oil

In mixing bowl, beat together egg whites, egg, 1 tablespoon chives, salt and pepper. Lightly coat bottom of skillet with non-stick spray. Sauté potatoes until golden. Add pepper, broccoli and water and cook covered about 3 minutes, until potatoes are tender. Uncover and cook until liquid has cooked away. Add oil to vegetables and toss until well-coated. Add egg mixture. Let cook until eggs begin to set, then stir well. Cover and continue cooking until eggs are set, but frittata is still moist on top. Remove cover and place under heated broiler until crisp and browned on top. Serve immediately topped with fresh chives.

*Cherish all your happy moments; they make
a fine cushion for old age.*
- Christopher Morley

Sautéed Tomatoes with Tarragon

Garnish with fresh tarragon.

2 large, ripe red tomatoes
1 T. butter
1 T. olive oil

1 T. fresh tarragon, chopped
freshly ground black pepper
to taste
dash of cayenne pepper

Slice tomatoes about 1/2-inch thick. Heat the butter and oil in a large iron skillet over medium heat. Add tomatoes and sprinkle with the spices. After 2 or 3 minutes the tomatoes should be brown. Flip them over and cook through.

*The more passions and desires one has,
the more ways one has of being happy.*
- Charlotte-Catherine

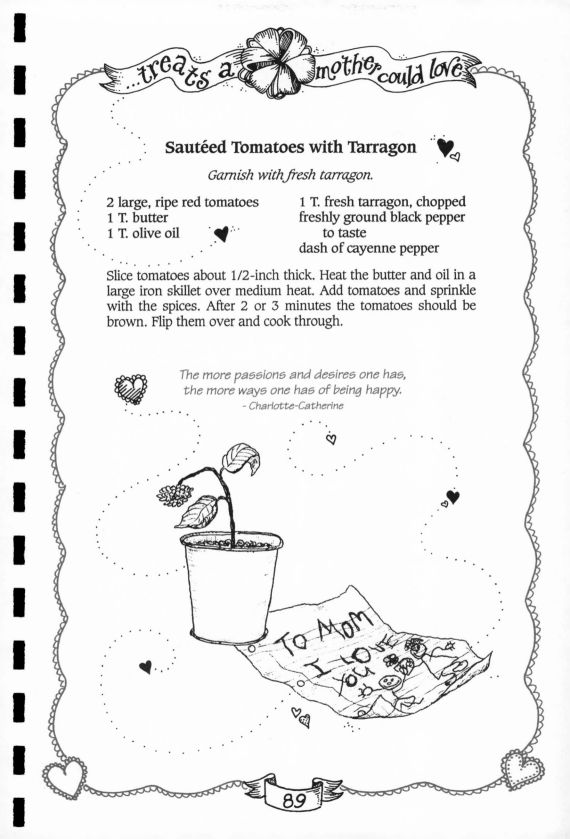

To Mom
I Love You

Herbal Omelet

Fresh garden herbs add a delicious taste to this special omelet.

2 T. butter
1/4 c. fresh mushrooms,
   sliced
5 eggs, beaten with 1 t.
   water
1/2 t. tarragon, chopped fine
1/2 t. fresh dill, chopped fine

1/2 t. fresh chives, chopped
   fine
salt & pepper to taste
1/2 red ripe tomato, chopped
1/4 c. cheddar cheese,
   shredded, plus more
   for top

Melt the butter in a large sauté pan over medium heat. Sauté the
mushrooms for one minute. In a large bowl, combine the eggs,
water, tarragon, dill, chives, salt and pepper and whisk into the
eggs briskly, for at least 30 seconds. When a drop of water siz-
zles in the pan, add the egg mixture. As the eggs set, gently run
a spatula through them several times so uncooked egg reaches
the bottom. Add tomato and cheese to the top of the omelet.
When the bottom is golden, flip half the omelet over on itself.
Transfer to a plate and sprinkle with more cheese. Garnish with
a sprig of dill.

Orange Muffins

Zesty and elegant. Place in a basket with a lace doily and fresh bouquet of daffodils.

1 3/4 c. flour, unsifted	1 large egg
1 1/2 t. baking powder	1 t. vanilla
1/2 t. salt	2/3 c. milk
6 T. butter, softened	2 to 3 T. grated orange rind
2/3 c. sugar	

Preheat oven to 375 degrees. Grease a muffin tin. In large bowl combine flour, baking powder and salt; set aside. In a mixing bowl beat together the butter and sugar at medium speed. Blend in egg and vanilla and beat until fluffy. Add flour mixture and milk alternately to this mixture, beating until just combined. Fold in orange rind. Bake for about 25 minutes, until tester comes out clean. Cool slightly and garnish with fresh violets.

Where there is great love, there are always miracles.
-Willa Cather

Strawberry Spinach Salad

Fresh and elegant!

8 c. fresh spinach leaves
1/2 c. fresh strawberries, halved
2 c. cantaloupe balls
2 T. seedless raspberry jam

2 T. raspberry white
    wine vinegar
1 T. honey
2 t. olive oil
1/4 c. macadamia nuts,
    chopped

In a large bowl, toss spinach, strawberries and cantaloupe. In a smaller bowl, whisk together jam, vinegar, honey and olive oil. Drizzle over salad and toss. Top with nuts. Serves 6.

Garnish a salad with strawberry fans. Cut four or five very thin slices through the berries from tip to hull, leaving the hull intact. Fan out the berries and arrange on the salad plate.

Mother's Luscious Chocolate Cake

Dust the top with powdered sugar over a lacy paper doily.
Leaves a beautiful image on top!

2 c. flour
2 t. baking soda
1/2 t. salt
1/2 c. butter
2 c. sugar
3 large eggs

1 1/2 t. vanilla
3 oz. unsweetened chocolate,
    melted and cooled
4 oz. pkg. instant chocolate
    pudding mix
1 c. sour cream
1/2 c. milk

Preheat oven to 350 degrees. Sift together the flour, baking soda and salt. In another larger bowl, beat together the butter and sugar; add eggs and beat until light and fluffy. Beat in the vanilla and chocolate. Alternating with the flour mixture, pudding mix and sour cream. Stir in the milk to thin batter. Pour into an 8-inch springform pan, and bake for 50 to 55 minutes or until cake tester comes out clean. Cool cake in pan for 10 minutes, then turn out onto rack and cool completely.

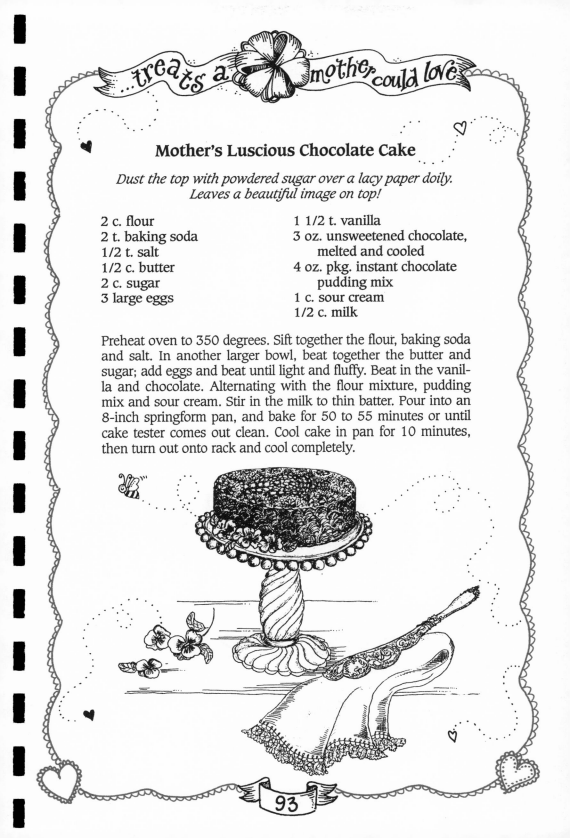

Almond Tea

Make a pot especially for Mom, to go with her chocolate cake.

3 regular tea bags
6 c. cold water
1 c. sugar or equivalent
   sweetener

2/3 c. lemon juice,
   freshly-squeezed
2 t. almond extract
1 t. vanilla extract

Place tea bags in 2 cups of boiling water for about 10 minutes. In a separate pan, bring 4 cups water to a boil and add sugar. Let simmer for 5 minutes, then add lemon, almond and vanilla. Combine the mixture with the tea. May be served hot or iced.

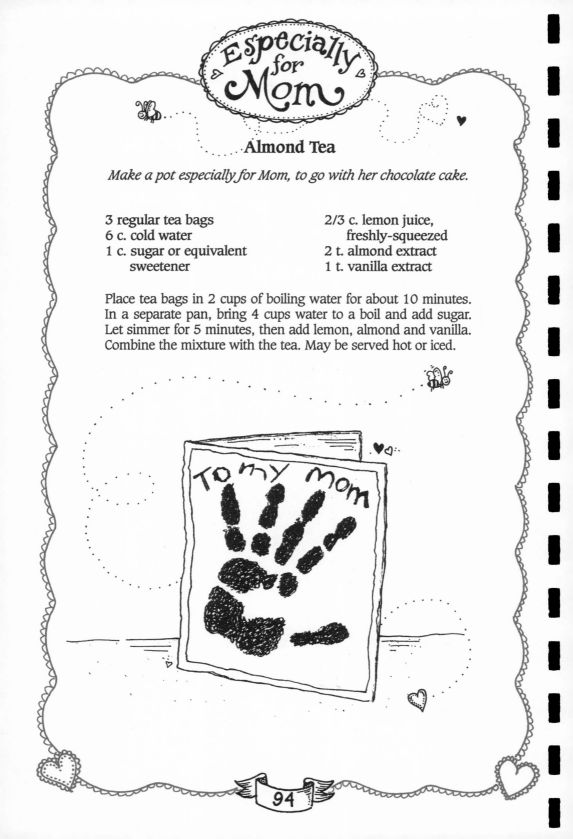

Gift ideas for Mother's Day...

Ivy Topiary

You will need:

2 small ivy plants
6" terra cotta pot
potting soil
twine

heavy-gauge wire
small pebbles
wire cutter
needle-nose pliers

Cut a strand of wire about 3 feet long. Bend the wire into a circle and use pliers to twist the ends together. The end piece should be about 5 inches long, or long enough to reach the bottom of the pot. Shape the loop into a circle. Put pebbles into the bottom of the pot, fill pot halfway with potting soil, and plant your ivies in the center of the pot. Make sure the shoots are growing outward in opposite directions. Cover the plants with additional soil and tap the pot to settle the roots. Water generously, allowing excess water to drain. Place your wire topiary form in the pot between the plants so it is firmly in the soil. Gently wrap the shoots around the twisted wire and onto both sides of the form. Temporarily tie the shoots in place with small pieces of twine. Then watch your topiary grow!

❤ Gift Coupon Book ❥

this coupon good for:
ONE DELICIOUS DINNER
Cooked by Me!

this coupon good for:
ONE WEED-FREE GARDEN
(til they grow back)

Help the kids give Mom or Grandma a special book of coupons they've made up just for her. Get out construction paper, magazines for picture cut-outs, markers and glue. Help them think of things they can do for Mother's Day, like wash the dishes, clean the fridge, make dinner, go shopping or weed the garden. Make each page into a "coupon" for the gift. (Include some coupons of your own if the gift is for your mother.)

Cookie Baking Box

Decorate the outside of a sturdy gift box with pretty fabric cut-outs coated with craft glue. Fill the box with cookie cutters, a recipe book like **Old-Fashioned Country Cookies**, sugar sprinkles, icing bag and tips and chocolate chips. A thoughtful gift for the mom who loves to bake!

Tea Basket

If your mother is a tea drinker, fill a basket with some teatime favorites...a special mug or cup, flavored and herbal tea bags, a silver teaspoon, sugar cubes or packets, even a tiny book of tea.

Lavender Dryer Sachet

A great gift for Mom...can also be used as a drawer or closet sachet. You'll need:

a piece of cotton fabric
needle and thread
string

lavender buds
cotton ball
decorative ribbon

Cut the fabric into a rectangle, double heart or double circle. With the fabric wrong side up, fold the edges over 1/4-inch and iron the edges flat. Fold the fabric in half to form your basic shape. Stitch all the way around the shape, leaving a small opening for stuffing. Turn the bag right side out and fill with as many lavender buds as possible, packing tightly. Place the cotton ball inside last, next to the opening, so no buds can escape. (For extra scent, you can put a drop of lavender oil on the cotton ball.) Stitch the opening shut...if you like, you can make a drawstring stitch so bag can be reopened. Make a bow with the ribbon and tie it to the sachet, sewing it on securely.

Garden Party

...seeds of friendship

Tomato Bruschetta
Raw Vegetables with Artichoke Dip
Sesame Asparagus
Minted Pea Salad
Greek Salad in a Pita Pocket
Violet Layer Cake
Cheesecake Cookies
Creamy Raspberry Smoothie

*Oh, such a commotion under the ground
When March called 'Ho, there, ho!'
...Then 'Ha! ha! ha!' a chorus came
Of laughter sweet and low
Of millions of flowers under the ground,
Yes, millions, beginning to grow.*
- Ralph Waldo Emerson

Garden Party

Tomato Bruschetta

Add thin slices of Vidalia or purple sweet onion before grilling.

12 oz. loaf Italian bread in 1"
    diagonal slices
1/2 pint cherry tomatoes, cut
    into fourths
1 small yellow pepper,
    chopped

3 T. olive oil
3 cloves garlic (1 minced, 2
    split in half)
1 T. fresh basil, chopped
2 T. Parmesan cheese, freshly
    grated

Place bread directly on grill (or on broiler rack in oven); lightly toast both sides about 2 minutes. In small bowl combine tomatoes, pepper, one tablespoon olive oil, minced garlic and basil. Rub one slice of each toasted bread slice with split garlic cloves and then brush with olive oil. Spoon heaping spoonfuls of tomato mixture onto each slice and sprinkle with cheese. Makes 8 servings.

A garden party is the perfect occasion for swapping seeds and cuttings. Give your guests each a little potted cutting as a party favor. If you want to encourage conversation, seat your guests at a round table, not too far apart.

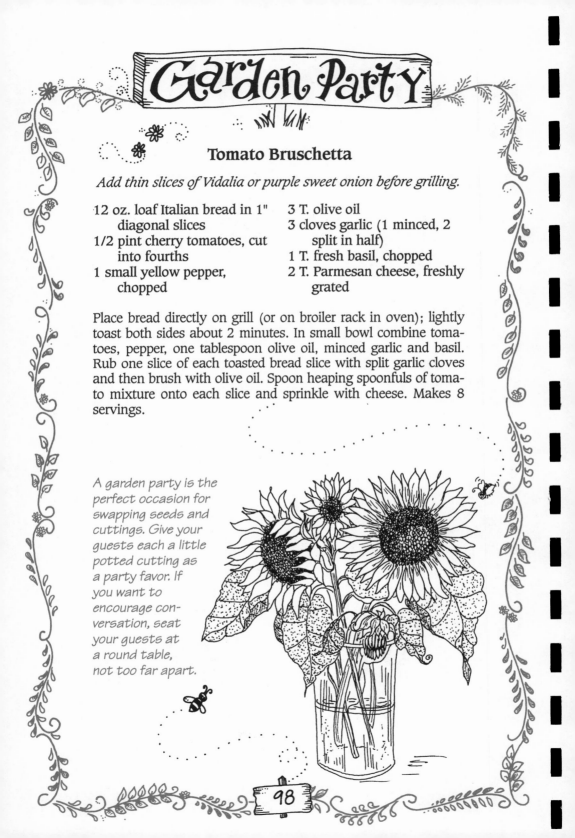

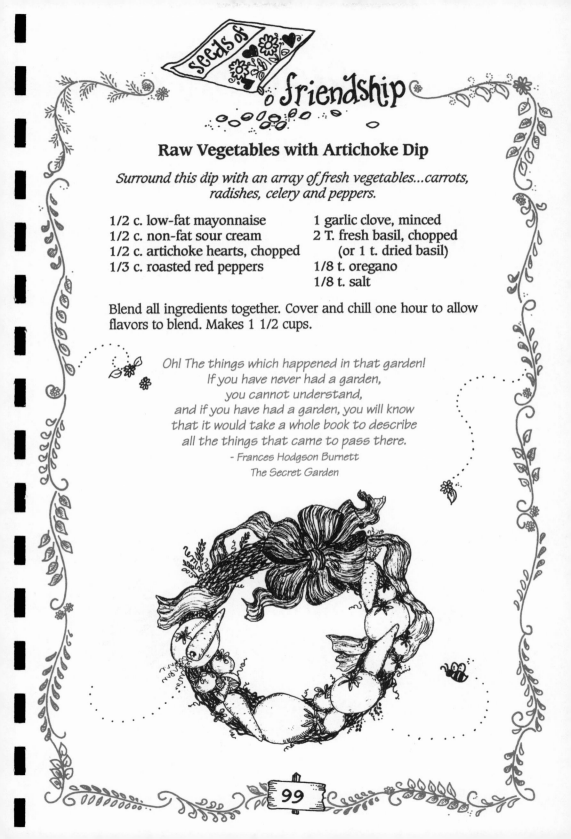

Raw Vegetables with Artichoke Dip

Surround this dip with an array of fresh vegetables...carrots, radishes, celery and peppers.

1/2 c. low-fat mayonnaise	1 garlic clove, minced
1/2 c. non-fat sour cream	2 T. fresh basil, chopped
1/2 c. artichoke hearts, chopped	(or 1 t. dried basil)
1/3 c. roasted red peppers	1/8 t. oregano
	1/8 t. salt

Blend all ingredients together. Cover and chill one hour to allow flavors to blend. Makes 1 1/2 cups.

Oh! The things which happened in that garden!
If you have never had a garden,
you cannot understand,
and if you have had a garden, you will know
that it would take a whole book to describe
all the things that came to pass there.
- Frances Hodgson Burnett
The Secret Garden

Sesame Asparagus

For best results, use an iron skillet. Serve chilled with a dash of fresh lemon juice.

1 lb. fresh asparagus, woody stalks
   broken off
2 T. peanut oil
2 T. shallots, minced

1 T. sesame seeds
2 t. soy sauce
freshly ground pepper
   to taste
dash of lemon juice

Heat a skillet over medium-high heat and add the peanut oil and the asparagus. Cook asparagus in a single layer for about 4 minutes, then turn and cook 3 more minutes. Asparagus will be slightly browned. Add the shallots and sesame seeds and cook, tossing the asparagus in the mixture, until the shallots are transparent. Add soy sauce and pepper, then transfer to a plate and sprinkle with lemon juice.

Asparagus is best when eaten freshly-picked. You can store for a few days in the refrigerator wrapped in a plastic bag. Don't clean until ready to cook.

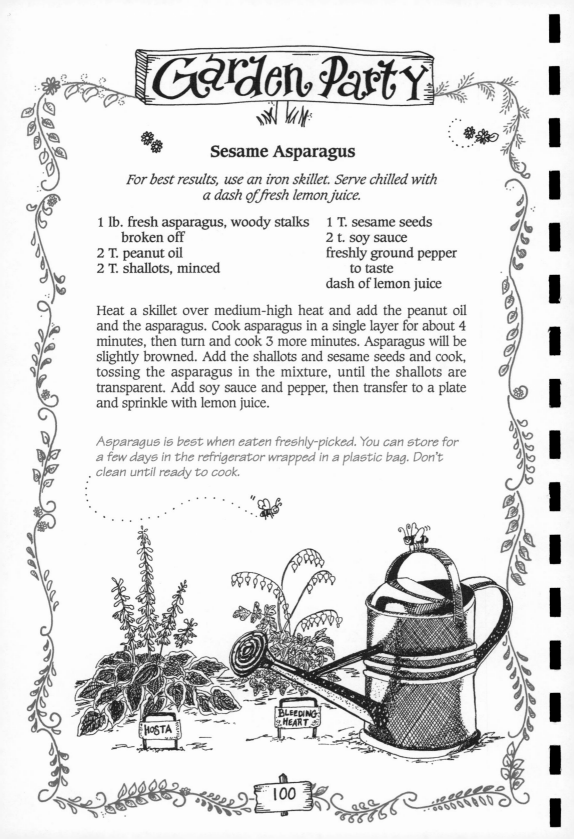

HOSTA

BLEEDING HEART

seeds of **friendship**

Minted Pea Salad

Can be prepared and served immediately or refrigerated.

4 c. fresh peas, blanched, or
    16 oz. bag frozen peas, thawed
1/4 lb. slice smoked ham, cooked
1/2 cup fresh mint leaves, chopped

1/2 c. mayonnaise
1/4 c. rice wine vinegar
1 t. fresh dill, chopped

Combine peas, ham and mint in mixing bowl. In another bowl, combine mayonnaise, vinegar and dill. Add dressing to peas and toss together.

> *They say spring has come when you can put*
> *your foot on three daisies.*
> *- Folk wisdom*

Garden Party

Greek Salad in a Pita Pocket

You can make a delicious sandwich out of 'most any vegetable salad with tasty pita bread.

4 rounds of pita bread, sliced horizontally and halved
crumbled feta cheese, to taste
fresh dill weed, chopped
1/2 t. dried oregano
1 sweet red bell pepper, sliced thin
1 t. crushed garlic

1/4 sweet red onion, sliced very thin
5 or 6 black Greek olives, pitted and sliced
1/2 ripe avocado, pitted and sliced
oil and vinegar salad dressing

Gently toss all salad ingredients in the dressing. Stuff into the pita pockets and enjoy! Serves 4.

friendship

Creamy Raspberry Smoothie

Cool, refreshing and colorful.

1 3/4 c. fresh raspberries
1 1/4 c. unsweetened white grape juice
1 1/2 c. raspberry sherbet
1/4 c. water

1 T. lemon juice
10 ice cubes
fresh mint sprigs
(optional)

Place raspberries and grape juice in blender and blend until smooth. Strain the mixture. Add sherbet, water, and lemon juice in blender container; cover and process until smooth. Add ice cubes; process until frothy. Garnish with fresh mint sprigs and serve immediately. Makes 3 cups.

About berries...

- Berries are best cleaned by rinsing gently in a colander using lukewarm water. Gently pat dry with a soft cloth.
- Be extra careful cleaning raspberries and blackberries, as they are very delicate.
- Leave the hull intact when you wash them.
- Don't wash berries until you're ready to serve them.
- If you can't use fresh berries immediately, line a large plate with a paper towel and arrange berries so they're not touching. They'll keep up to three days, although refrigerating does cause berries to lose some of their flavor.

Garden Party

Violet Layer Cake

Freshly-picked violets look pretty around the base of the cake.

White cake:

1/2 c. butter, softened
1 2/3 c. sugar
2 1/2 c. cake flour, sifted
1/4 t. salt

1 1/4 c. cold water
1 t. vanilla extract
4 egg whites, beaten
2 t. baking powder

Cream butter and sugar with a mixer. Sift flour and salt together and add to butter mixture, alternating with water. Add vanilla. In a separate bowl, beat egg whites until frothy and add baking powder gradually, continuing to beat until stiff. Fold egg whites into the batter. Pour into two greased and floured 8-inch layer pans and bake at 350 degrees for 25 minutes. Touch center of cake to test for doneness; when it springs back, it is done.

Buttercream frosting:

1/2 c. butter, softened
1 1/2 c. powdered sugar

2 T. milk
1/2 t. vanilla extract

Beat all ingredients together with a mixer until smooth and thick. Add more sugar if frosting is too thin. Frost both layers of cake and stack.

Frosted Violets:

With a small artist's brush, gently brush a mixture of egg white and water on freshly cleaned and dried violet blossoms. Dip in superfine sugar. Scatter frosted violets over the top of the cake.

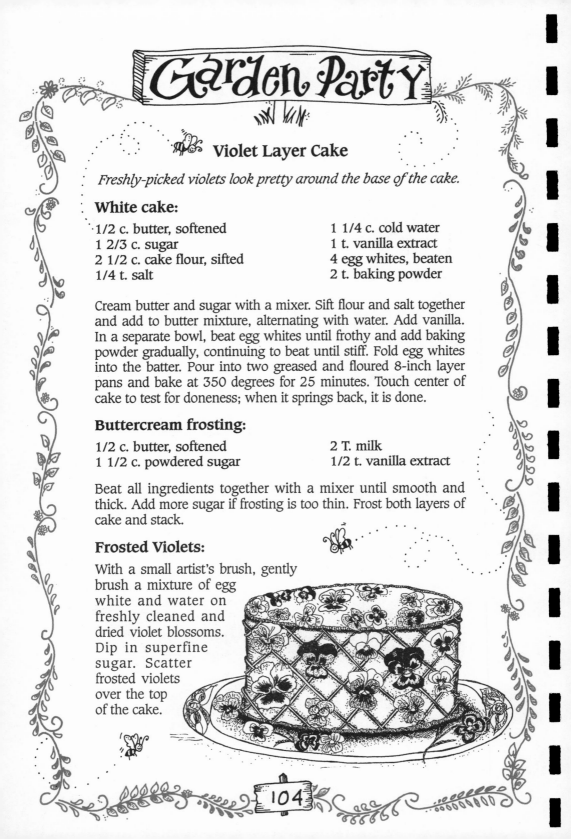

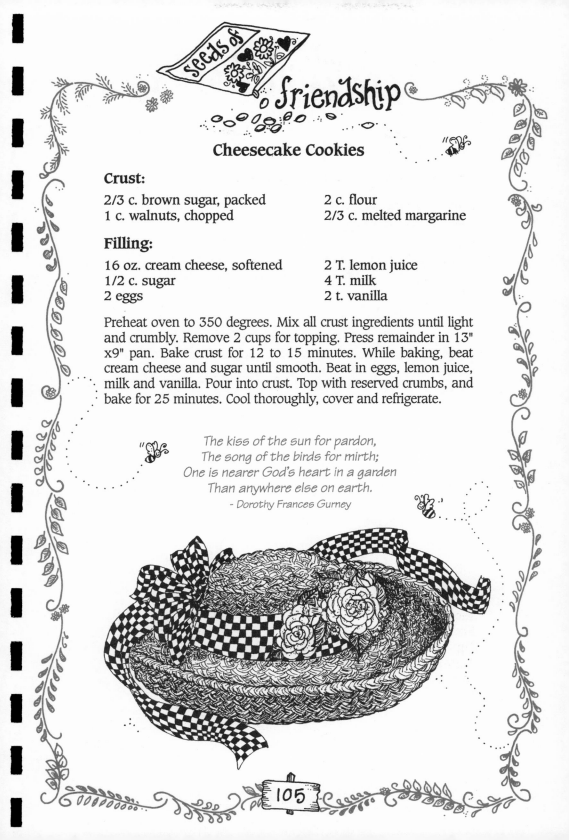

seeds of friendship

Cheesecake Cookies

Crust:

2/3 c. brown sugar, packed
1 c. walnuts, chopped

2 c. flour
2/3 c. melted margarine

Filling:

16 oz. cream cheese, softened
1/2 c. sugar
2 eggs

2 T. lemon juice
4 T. milk
2 t. vanilla

Preheat oven to 350 degrees. Mix all crust ingredients until light and crumbly. Remove 2 cups for topping. Press remainder in 13" x9" pan. Bake crust for 12 to 15 minutes. While baking, beat cream cheese and sugar until smooth. Beat in eggs, lemon juice, milk and vanilla. Pour into crust. Top with reserved crumbs, and bake for 25 minutes. Cool thoroughly, cover and refrigerate.

The kiss of the sun for pardon,
The song of the birds for mirth;
One is nearer God's heart in a garden
Than anywhere else on earth.
- Dorothy Frances Gurney

Garden Party

Fresh Ideas...

Floral Spoons

Collect pretty, deep-bowled spoons and ladles from flea markets to make this easy craft. They make beautiful party favors! You'll need:

old spoons
florist's foam
craft tacky glue
thin satin ribbon

small dried flower blossoms
such as purple statice,
baby's breath, globe amaranth
and lavender

Cut a small amount of florist's foam to fill the well of the spoon. (A melon-baller works perfectly to cut the foam for a regular tablespoon.) Glue foam firmly into the spoon and let dry completely, overnight if possible. When dry, push dried flowers into the base, completely covering the foam. Tie a bow onto the spoon handle. Place spoons at individual place settings.

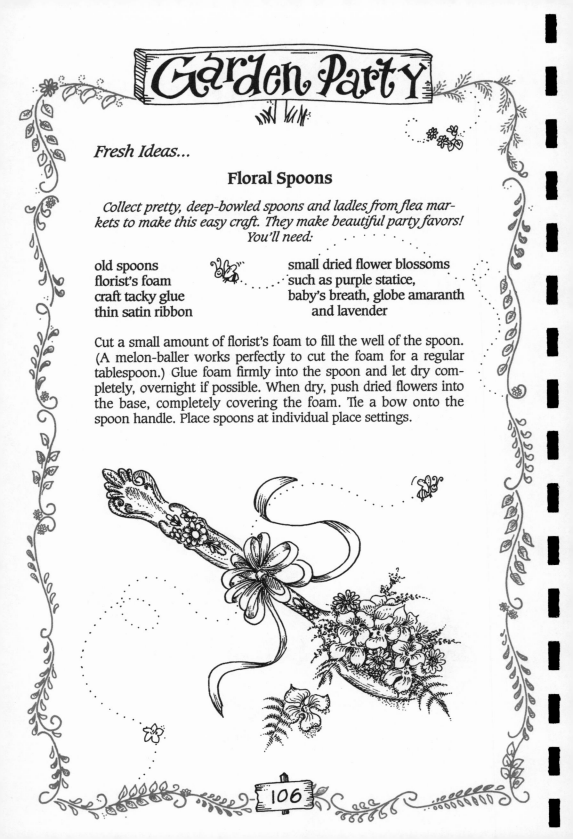

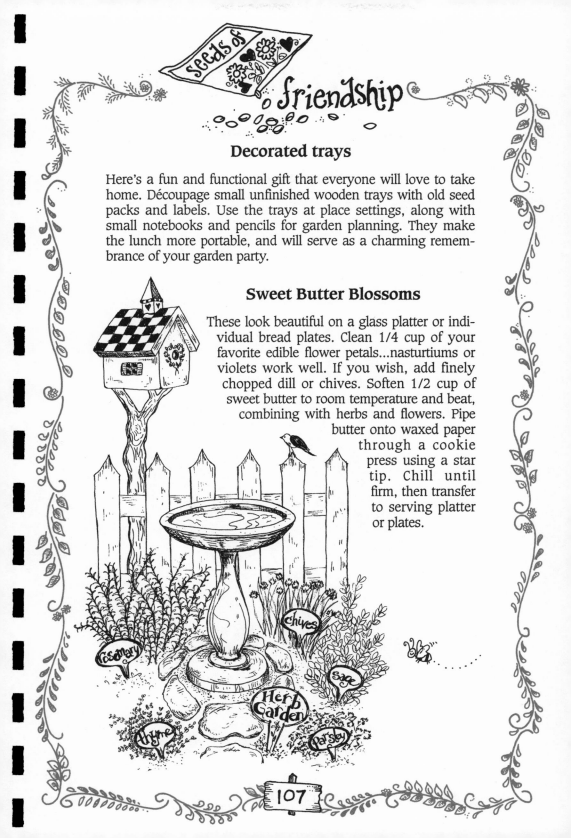

Decorated trays

Here's a fun and functional gift that everyone will love to take home. Découpage small unfinished wooden trays with old seed packs and labels. Use the trays at place settings, along with small notebooks and pencils for garden planning. They make the lunch more portable, and will serve as a charming remembrance of your garden party.

Sweet Butter Blossoms

These look beautiful on a glass platter or individual bread plates. Clean 1/4 cup of your favorite edible flower petals...nasturtiums or violets work well. If you wish, add finely chopped dill or chives. Soften 1/2 cup of sweet butter to room temperature and beat, combining with herbs and flowers. Pipe butter onto waxed paper through a cookie press using a star tip. Chill until firm, then transfer to serving platter or plates.

Garden Party

Forced Hyacinths

Forcing hyacinths was such a popular practice in Victorian days, special hyacinth glasses were made just for that purpose and can be found in many antique shops. Forcing is easy to do; just be sure you get good quality bulbs and keep them in a cool place (damp sand is perfect) until ready to plant. Choose a container that will support the bulb slightly above the water and have plenty of room for the roots; if you can't find a real hyacinth glass, a bud vase, jelly jar or little glass pitcher will usually work well. Fill with lukewarm water, making sure the water just touches the bottom of the bulb. Change the water about twice a week. Keep in a cool, dark place for three or four weeks or until roots and leaves begin to show. Then move to a warmer, sunnier spot. Turn the container occasionally for even sunlight exposure. Hyacinths take about six weeks to blossom, so be patient!

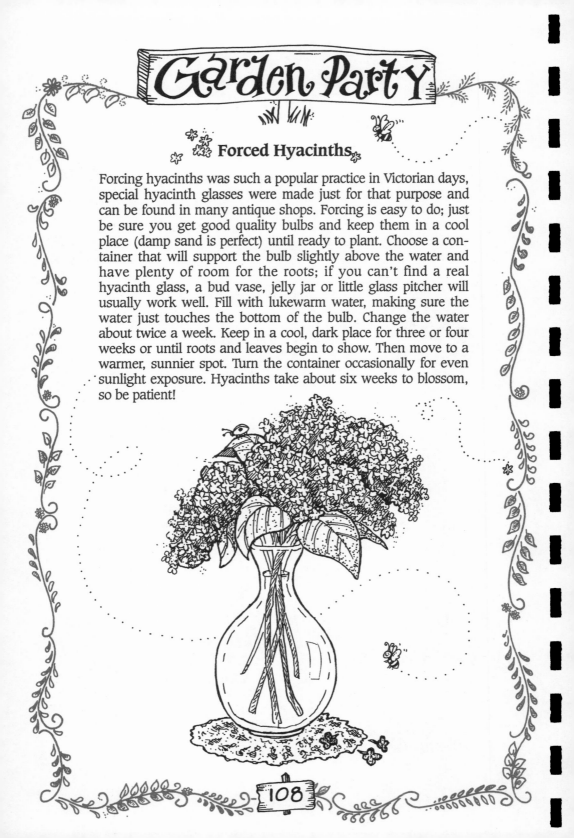

Heavenly Herbal Luncheon

...thyme for special friends

Basil Tomato Bisque
Beggar's Purses
Poached Salmon
Rosemary Chicken Salad
Cucumber-Yogurt Salad
Rotini with Feta, Tomatoes and Olives

*Gently steep our spirits, carrying with them
dreams of flowers.*
- William Wordsworth

Please touch
the herbs

Basil-Tomato Bisque

Top with fresh chopped basil and buttered croutons.

2 lbs. ripe, red tomatoes (or
   2-15 oz. cans tomatoes),
   chopped
1 onion, sliced thin
1 T. butter
1 bay leaf
1 T. dark brown sugar
4 t. fresh basil, chopped fine

2 whole cloves
1 t. salt
1/2 t. black pepper
1 pt. cream
1 c. milk
1 c. croutons, buttered and
   browned

Peel tomatoes by blanching briefly in boiling water; remove skin and seeds and chop. Sauté onion in butter and add tomatoes, bay leaf, brown sugar, 2 teaspoons basil, cloves, salt and pepper. Simmer 20-30 minutes. Remove bay leaf and cloves and puree mixture in a blender. Strain, then add cream and milk and heat slowly over medium heat. Garnish with croutons and a sprinkle of fresh basil. Serves 6.

Beggar's Purses

You can find morels, the little tree-shaped mushrooms, in Michigan and Ohio woods in early spring, hiding under elm trees and may apples. (Always be sure the mushrooms you find are edible!)

1 c. morel mushrooms, cleaned and sliced
1 t. garlic, minced
1 T. butter
1/4 c. Madeira wine
1 T. chives, chopped

1/2 c. wild rice, cooked
4 sheets phyllo dough, thawed
4 T. sweet butter, melted
leek tops, cut into 4 ribbons and blanched

Sauté mushrooms and garlic in 1 tablespoon butter. Add wine and bring to a boil. Simmer until wine has evaporated. Stir in chives and let cool a bit. Stir in rice and set aside. Brush one sheet of phyllo with melted butter and top with second sheet of pastry. Brush second sheet with butter. Continue layering phyllo, brushing each sheet with butter. Cut pastry in quarters, forming four rectangles. Spoon mushroom filling in the center of each rectangle. Bring up all sides of each rectangle and tie with a leek ribbon, so it looks like a bundle or package. Brush all sides of the bundles with melted butter. Place on a baking sheet and bake at 425 degrees for 8 to 10 minutes, or until brown and crisp. Unbaked bundles can be made ahead of time and refrigerated, covered, up to six hours.

Herbal Luncheon

Poached Salmon

Serve on an elegant platter with dill sauce.

4-6 oz. pieces of fresh salmon, wrapped in parchment paper
Court bouillon (recipe follows)
Dill sauce (recipe follows)

In a large saucepan, cover wrapped salmon with court bouillon. Cook in boiling water for about 8 minutes. Remove salmon from liquid and remove paper carefully.

Court Bouillon:

1 c. celery, chopped
1 c. onion, chopped
1 t. black peppercorns
2 T. fresh parsley, chopped

2 T. fresh tarragon, chopped
2 c. vermouth
1/2 lemon
1 t. salt

Combine all ingredients in a medium saucepan and bring to a boil. Reduce heat and simmer for 8 minutes.

Dill Sauce:

1 c. sour cream
1 c. mayonnaise
2 T. fresh dill, chopped

2 T. lemon juice
salt and pepper to taste

Combine all ingredients in a blender and blend until smooth.

For a delicious addition to homemade soups, try adding fresh dill sprigs instead of celery leaves.

Rosemary Chicken Salad

Can be prepared ahead of time and refrigerated until your luncheon.

3 c. cooked chicken breast, cubed	1/3 c. sour cream
3 c. celery, thinly sliced	1 T. fresh rosemary,
1/3 c. mayonnaise	finely chopped

Combine chicken and celery. In a separate bowl, blend mayonnaise, sour cream and rosemary. Blend chicken with dressing and mix until well coated. Makes 4 servings.

Make a double batch of pesto and freeze some in an ice cube tray; then seal the cubes in a plastic freezer bag until you need them to enhance pastas, breads and chicken dishes.

Cucumber-Yogurt Salad

Cool and refreshing. Add radish roses for a pretty garnish.

2 cucumbers, peeled, halved and seeded
1 c. plain low-fat yogurt
1 T. olive oil
2 t. white wine vinegar

salt and freshly ground pepper to taste
2 T. fresh mint leaves, chopped
4 radish roses (see below)
fresh mint sprigs for garnish

Cut cucumbers into crescents. Lay on paper towels, sprinkle with salt and refrigerate for an hour to remove excess liquid. Combine the yogurt, oil, vinegar, salt and pepper and mint. Pat the cucumbers dry and toss them in the dressing. Garnish with radishes and mint.

To make radish roses, slice off the ends of the radishes. Score one end of each radish about 3/4 of the way through, cutting the radish in a criss-cross pattern. Place in ice water for about 20 minutes to open.

Rotini with Feta, Tomatoes and Olives

Serve with warm crusty bread.

1/4 c. extra virgin olive oil
28 oz. can crushed tomatoes
1 c. black olives,
    sliced and drained
1 c. feta cheese,
    crumbled
16 oz. rotini pasta,
    cooked

Heat olive oil in a
large skillet. Stir in
the tomatoes, olives
and cheese and heat
through. Add pasta to tomato
mixture and toss well. Makes 4
servings.

There are many imported olives you can try in pastas and salads...huge, meaty Alfonsos, sharp and spicy Sicilians and flavorful Ligurias from Italy; rich Calamatas and Royals from Greece; tender, savory Nicoise and crisp Picholines from France...ask to try a variety of olives at your local gourmet deli.

Herbal Luncheon

Herb-stuffed Chicken Breasts

Select an herbal spread from the dairy case or make your own with a mixture of cream cheese, tarragon, chives and parsley.

12 sheets phyllo
2 T. butter, melted

4 chicken breasts, thinly
    pounded
1/2 c. herb cheese spread,
    prepared

Preheat oven to 400 degrees. Place one sheet of phyllo dough on work surface and brush with butter. Put another sheet on top, and brush again with butter. Place third sheet on top. Set aside, cover with damp cloth (to keep dough moist,) and repeat above steps 3 more times. Spread one quarter of the herb cheese spread onto the end of each phyllo pile and roll dough, placing seam side down. Fold phyllo around each chicken breast and brush with margarine. Place seam side down and bake until phyllo is golden and chicken is tender.

Phyllo Tip: Thaw frozen phyllo dough in the refrigerator a day before using. Also remember to keep dough covered with plastic wrap, waxed paper or a damp towel. This will keep the dough from drying out. It is much easier to work with moist dough.

thyme for special friends

Herbalisms...

Herb Brushes

☆ You can easily make herb brushes for flavoring grilled foods. All you need are bunches of freshly-picked herb sprigs. Fasten a bunch of herbs to a twig or the handle of a wooden spoon and tie the stems together with twine. Dip in olive or vegetable oil and baste your chicken, fish or steaks. Some excellent savory herbs are: thyme, sage, cilantro, oregano, chervil, dill, chives, basil, parsley, rosemary, mint and lavender.

Herb & Spice Butter Logs

Try combining softened sweet butter with herb and spice combinations; roll into logs with waxed paper and refrigerate until hard. Delicious on fresh breads, sweet corn, broiled salmon and potatoes. Experiment with different combinations...dill with lemon and paprika; rosemary with mint; chives with freshly ground pepper; tarragon with lemon; basil with garlic, oregano and pine nuts. Just slice off the butter in rounds to serve. Remember, a little goes a long way!

Herbal Luncheon

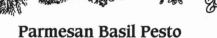

Parmesan Basil Pesto

A delicious, savory sauce for pasta, toasted bread rounds (crostini), pizza and roast chicken.

4 cloves garlic, minced
2 c. clean basil leaves
1/3 c. extra virgin olive oil
1/4 c. Parmesan cheese,
    freshly grated

3 T. pine nuts or walnuts,
    crushed
freshly ground pepper to taste

Combine garlic with fresh basil and olive oil. Process in a food processor until the basil is puréed. Add Parmesan cheese and nuts. Season with pepper. Keep in a covered jar in the refrigerator until ready to use. Makes 3/4 cup.

...for there is no friend like a sister,
In calm or stormy weather;
To cheer one on the tedious way,
To fetch one if one goes astray...
- Christina Rossetti

Herb-Infused Vinegars

A tall, pretty glass bottle of vinegar makes a lovely gift when a few leaves or stalks of freshly picked herbs are added. Choose white, cider or wine vinegar. Add tarragon and chives, rosemary and garlic, lavender, orange and mint or basil and oregano. Experiment to find just the right combination for salads and marinades.

Healing Herbal Teas

Try these traditional herbal teas for garden-variety ailments...you may find they work as well as synthetic medicine.

Lavender ....headaches
Thyme.......................................hay fever
Purple sage ....sore throat
Chamomile..............................stuffy nose, upset
　　　　　　　　　　　　　　　　stomach, insomnia
Peppermint ....indigestion
Lavender and rosemary ....when you're feeling blue

Herbal Luncheon

Herbal Housekeeping

Herbal recipes for housekeeping have been handed down for generations, and you can still use them today. Herbs are economical and earth-friendly. Here are just a few natural remedies.

Herbal Vinegar Cleaner:
Fill a mason jar three-quarters full with white vinegar and add some herbs such as basil or lemon verbena from your garden. Let it sit in a sunny spot for a few days and then strain. Use herbal vinegar from a spray bottle to clean your oven and make windows sparkle. For windows, dilute a few tablespoons of vinegar in a quart of water. Use newspapers instead of paper towels.

Lemon Balm Polish:
Simply wrap lemon balm leaves in a clean piece of cheesecloth to polish wood furniture. The oil also acts to keep cats away from furniture.

Cinnamon Air Freshener:
A quick and easy cinnamon recipe will erase stale cooking odors. Simply stir a few teaspoons of ground cinnamon into two cups of hot water and let simmer for awhile on the stove.

"Soap" for Fine Washables:
Use soapwort leaves, crushed and mixed with hot water and then strained, to make a gentle fabric wash. Especially nice for silk fabrics.

Tansy Pest Repellent:
Repel flies, fleas, and ants with little muslin bags filled with tansy leaves. To keep mosquitoes away, use leaves of pennyroyal. And to repel moths, make bags of lavender, basil, rosemary or peppermint leaves. Hang the bags in your closets.

A Guide to Popular Herbs

Basil - Brings out the flavor of tomatoes. Used to make pesto; also good in potato and rice salads.

Bay leaves - Used whole in many soups and stews; then removed before serving.

Chives - Add an onion flavor to omelets, soups and steamed vegetables.

Cilantro - Otherwise known as "Mexican parsley," has a hot, spicy, minty flavor. Sprinkle fresh leaves on spicy Mexican and Indian dishes.

Dill - A delicate yet pungent flavor that is perfect in potato and chicken soups, egg and potato salads, and sprinkled on cucumbers and steamed carrots. Also wonderful in breads.

Garlic - The mainstay of most Italian and Greek dishes; whole heads can be roasted and the soft cloves spread on breads, or cloves can be simmered to flavor soups and sauces. Crushed garlic is used in many salads and stir-fry dishes and on grilled steaks, chicken and fish.

Lavender - Flavors jams, jellies and vinegars; steep the flowers for a comforting tea.

Lemongrass - Is used in many Thai dishes. Has a fresh lemony taste that complements many soup dishes.

Marigold flowers - Their peppery flavor will spice up a sauce or a salad. Also good in baked fish dishes.

Marjoram - A mild herb, slightly sweet, good on fresh sliced tomatoes, omelets or meat dishes.

Nasturtiums - The flowers are beautiful in salads and have a slightly sweet, peppery taste.

Oregano - Used to enrich the flavor of tomato sauces and many Italian dishes. A pungent, dusky flavor.

Peppermint - Perfect as a soothing tea, in fruit salads and cake recipes.

Rosemary - Used in many Greek and Italian dishes as a flavoring for marinades and salad dressings.

Sage - Perfect for flavoring the stuffing for your Thanksgiving turkey; used in many pork and chicken dishes as well.

Tarragon - Used as a flavoring for vinegars, in salads and chicken dishes.

Index

tulips & daffodils robin's eggs tiny buds mushroom hunting apple blossoms fresh earth leprechauns lavender rosemary seed packets rake & hoe spring fever tea parties April showers Easter baskets graduation

Gooseberry Patch Originals

WELCOME HOME for the HOLIDAYS
your companion from September through December

Welcome Home For The Holidays

Go from harvest through Christmas... a treasury of holiday recipes, decorating tips, traditions & easy-to-make gifts

Old-Fashioned Country Christmas

A holiday keepsake of recipes, traditions, homemade gifts, decorating ideas, & favorite childhood memories.

OLD-FASHIONED COUNTRY COOKIES
hundreds of recipes, tips, & ideas

Old-Fashioned Country Cookies

Yummy recipes, tips, traditions, how-to's, and sweet memories... everything Cookies!

OLD-FASHIONED COUNTRY CHRISTMAS
our all-time BEST SELLER!

GOOD FOR YOU!
recipes, fun ideas, heartwarming stories, good for body, mind, soul

For Bees & Me

FOR BEES & ME
garden-fresh recipes, backyard entertaining & gifts from the garden

A Bouquet of Garden-Fresh Recipes, Memories, Hints, Simple Pleasures, Herbal Beauty, Pet Care, Backyard Entertainment & Easy-to-Make Gifts

Good For You!

A collection of good food, good fun, & good stories for the body, mind, & soul!

tulips & daffodils ☙ robin's eggs ❧ tiny buds

mushroom hunting ❧ apple blossoms ❧ fresh earth ❧ leprechauns ❧ lavender

Easter baskets

graduation ❧ spring fever ❧ tea parties

April showers ❧ seed packets ❧ rake & hoe ❧ rosemary

GOOSEBERRY PATCH
P.O. Box 190, Dept. CELS
Delaware, OH 43015

A Country Store In Your Mailbox®

Please send me the following Gooseberry Patch books:

Book	Quantity	Price	Total
Old-Fashioned Country Christmas		$14.95	
Welcome Home for the Holidays		$14.95	
Old-Fashioned Country Cookies		$14.95	
For Bees & Me		$17.95	
Good For You!		$14.95	
Homespun Christmas		$14.95	
Celebrate Spring		$12.95	
Celebrate Summer		$12.95	
Celebrate Autumn		$12.95	
Celebrate Winter		$12.95	
		Merchandise Total	
		Ohio Residents add 6 1/4%	

Shipping & handling: Add $2.50 for each book. Call for special delivery prices.

Quantity discounts and special shipping prices available when purchasing
6 or more books. Call and ask! Wholesale inquiries invited.

Total

Name: _____

Address: _____

City: _____ State: _____ Zip: _____

We accept checks, money orders, Visa or MasterCard (please include expiration date). Payable in U.S. funds only. Prices subject to change.

GOOSEBERRY PATCH
P.O. Box 190, Dept. CELS
Delaware, OH 43015

A Country Store In Your Mailbox®

♡ How to Order ♡
For faster service on credit card orders,
call toll-free 1·800·85·GOOSE!
(1·800·854·6673)

Please send me the following Gooseberry Patch books:

Book	Quantity	Price	Total
Old-Fashioned Country Christmas		$14.95	
Welcome Home for the Holidays		$14.95	
Old-Fashioned Country Cookies		$14.95	
For Bees & Me		$17.95	
Good For You!		$14.95	
Homespun Christmas		$14.95	
Celebrate Spring		$12.95	
Celebrate Summer		$12.95	
Celebrate Autumn		$12.95	
Celebrate Winter		$12.95	
		Merchandise Total	
		Ohio Residents add 6 1/4%	

Shipping & handling: Add $2.50 for each book. Call for special delivery prices.

Quantity discounts and special shipping prices available when purchasing
6 or more books. Call and ask! Wholesale inquiries invited.

Total

Name: _____

Address: _____

City: _____ State: _____ Zip: _____

We accept checks, money orders, Visa or MasterCard (please include expiration date). Payable in U.S. funds only. Prices subject to change.

tulips & daffodils 🪺robin's eggs 🌱tiny buds 🌿mushroom hunting 🍎apple blossoms ⚒fresh earth🌸 leprechauns🌿 lavender🌾 rosemary 🪻seed packets🌱 rake & hoe 🌱 April showers 🫖tea parties 🌞spring fever 🌱graduation 🐰Easter baskets🌿